MW00450447

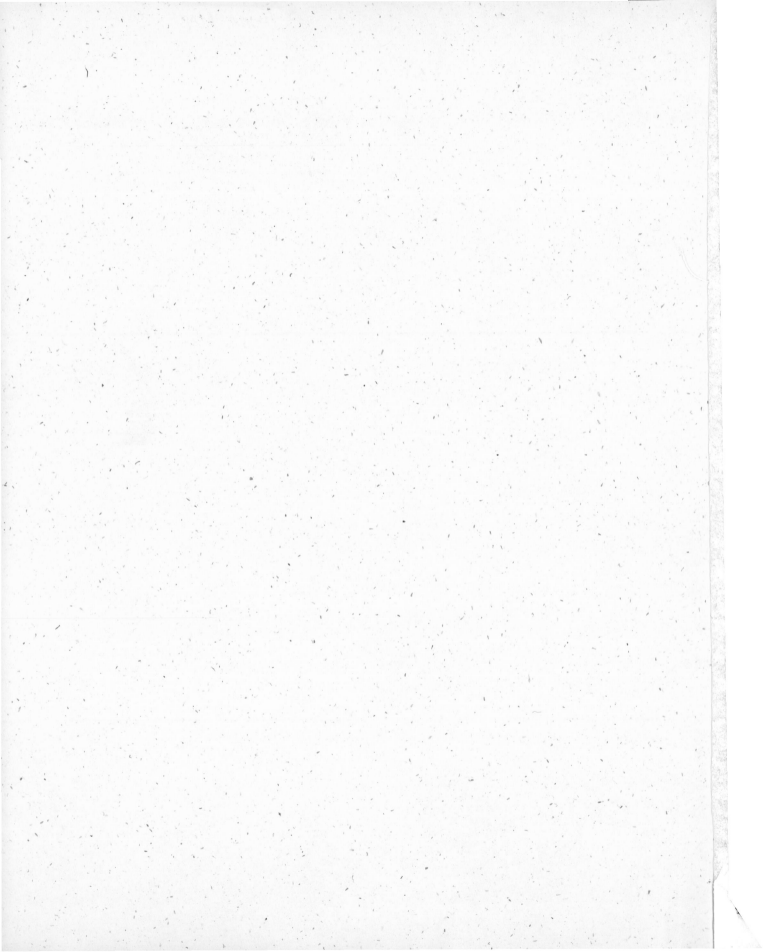

Born to Slow Horses

ALSO BY KAMAU BRATHWAITE

Bibliography

Caribbean Man in Space & Time
Our Ancestral Heritage: A Bibliography of the Roots of Colture in the English-Speaking Caribbean
Barbados Poetry: A Checklist. Slavery to the Present
Jamaica Poetry: A Checklist. Slavery to the Present

Biographical Material

The Zea Mexican Diary (ZMD)
The Poet & His Place in Barbadian Culture
Barbajan Poems
Trench Town Rock (TTR)
ConVERSations with Nathaniel Mackay
Golokwati 2000

Culture Studies

Folk Culture of the Slaves in Jamaica
The Development of Creole Society in Jamaica, 1770–1820
Contradictory Omens
Wars of Respect: Nanny Sam Sharpe and the Struggle for People's Liberation
Bajan Culture: Report and Plan
Afternoon of the Status Crow
Gods of the Middle Passage
The Colonial Encounter: Language/University of Mysore Lectures
History of the Voice
Kamau Monograph
MR Magical Realism
Missile & Capsule

History

The People Who Came

Literary Criticism & Commentary

History of the Voice: The Development of Nation Language in the Anglophone Caribbean
Roots
Three Caribbean Poets [Brathwaite, Goodison, Mervyn Morris]

Plays

Four Plays for Primary Schools
Odale's Choice
How Music Came to the Ainchan People

Poetry

Rights of Passage
Masks
Islands
Penguin Modern Poets 15
Days & Nights
Other Exiles
Poetry '75 International
Black + Blues
Mother Poem
Soweto
Word Making Man: Poem for Nicolás Guillén in Xaymaca
Sun Poem
Third World Poems
Jah Music
Korabra
Le détonateur de visibilité/The Visibility Trigger
X/Self [X/S]
Sappho Sakyl's Meditations
Shar/Hurricane Poem
Middle Passages
Words Need Love Too

Prosefiction & Dream Stories

Letter from Cambridge
The Black Angel
Law & Order
Christine
Cricket
4th Traveller
Meridian
Dream Chad
I Cristobál Colon
Scapeghosts
Dream Haiti
Dream Stories [DS]
Y Cristobál Kamau
Dream Orange
The Dream Sycorax Letter
Mmusiowaatuunaa (for Tom Dent)
My Funny Valentine
Film Studies
Astúrias
Grease

BORN to SLOW HO

Kamau Brathwaite

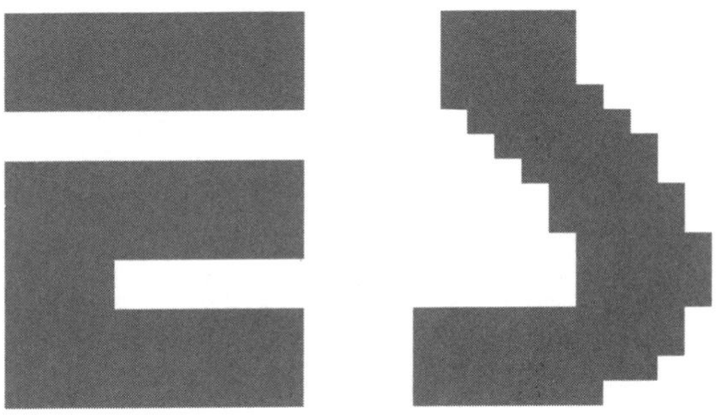

Wesleyan University Press · Middletown, Connecticut

Published by Wesleyan University Press, Middletown, CT 06459

www.wesleyan.edu/wespress

Printed in the United States of America

Second printing, 2006

Production by BW&A Books, Inc.

Library of Congress Cataloging-in-Publication Data

Brathwaite, Kamau, 1930–

Born to slow horses / Kamau Brathwaite.

p. cm. — (Wesleyan poetry)

ISBN 0–8195–6745–0 (cloth : alk. paper)

1. West Indies — Poetry. 2. West Indians — Foreign countries — Poetry. I. Title. II. Series.

PR9230.9.B68B67 2005

811'.54—dc22 2004043091

for

Dream Chad

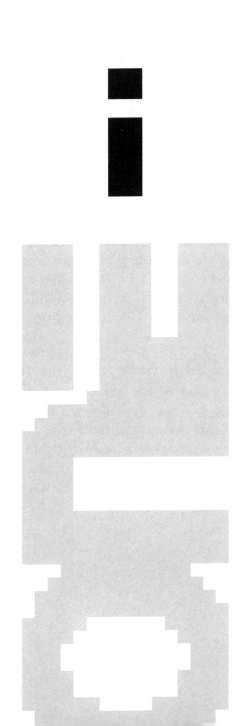

THE MASTER OF THE MARY JONES

for the pupil, age 12, who painted all this at the Village College, Bottisham, Cambridge
and hailin up Dylan Thomas' innocence & Ernest Hemingway's novella about my own BrownsBeach sea

Fling of his wish have caught the sea
capture the blue and the green
conquer the flash and flail of the tail
the will of the rainbow fish .
Hold him still in his sky blue eyes
till the trail foam flow like white
cross birds out of the net web tides

He have fish so lost in these green
back cloths. that the fan shape vanishing tails
had stitch in his mind. a huge unaccountable fish
which bubble-up inna de middaday-blink. in sun into a thousand eyes
and at night it lie on a milk white
way under the bright tip tides .
fish of his wish and his failure to catch . out of the silk song sea

All night he have fallow the tall tail
swim of the star back fish
till the black cloth dark drown its milky eyes
under the last star bows and dawn up the stem is white
and the swimmming wind and the sail bright tides
are free of the watch-night singing sea
and the broad back fathoms greem

F*or what have he watch in the fish*
cold night. sewing leviathans into his eyes .
for what have e wish in his deep fishing dream for the white
reed hair of the tugging bottomless tides?
He have sail so long and have sea-
saw, sea-watch, silently sit, waiting the green
back fathomless fish to cross his traps with its tail

B*ut morning had clear the stars from his eyes*
and he see in the pillow white
slip & sheet of the spread out tides
no monster afloat on the silk song sea
but the bump and bubbelling backs of the green
whale waves. no flickering tails
but the snow drop dots of surfacing pilot fish

S*o im wishes still trail in the snow white*
trough and his haul is a empty tide
that ebbing and flowing follow the sun round sea .
But the fisherman sit in im green
leaf wood and fashion again tall tales
in the mid-day-maddening sun . till im see the fish
in the silk torn wake staring with sum shot eyes

It have come to his hail from the wish web tides
out of the wood and the wave leaf watch
of his lonely fisherman's sea
and that night it is scale with the Milky Way . green
star flame and blue fish foam . and its tale
it make of the night watch bumps of smaller travelling fish
harbouring under the boat . and its sailing eyes
is the night wick moon and the water star strike bright

At last he wd drag his wish from the sea
tackle the moon and cut down green
leave sun . blue boy again in the fan tail
day of his dream come true in the fathomless fish
catch in his all night eyes .
At last he cd turn in the rain blue white
of his foam joy haul and bird sail home on the tides

>

BERMUDAS

marine to noon on AméricasAirplane

First the dark meer
begins to breathe gently into green
into light & light green
until there are like blue

ribs upon the water. dreaming
and the ribs of water's colour are the gills
of the first fish breathing
the first land the first eye

-lann
until there is what shd not be here
on the water
white

footsteps of sand from the bottom of the ocean
become the thin road to Eleuthera
long & thin upon the water walking
until there is suddenly a black stone

a dark
veil kabala surrounding by whorls
of worship green water scallops
folding into themselves like soft

jewels the first huge fish
out of creation
w/ribs veins glimpse
of a tail & deep channels in between

where they will be mountains & ridges
& villages & ozure indigo sunsets
of lapis lazuli & white salt marking its finely corrugated edges
& stretching out into thousands of tongues. miles

of soft drifting labials. like pellucid love
on the water. this fish
from the air of so many so many untangles
& 10 thousand years later there are trees

glistening sunlight & listening rain & white streets
& houses & people walkin bout & talkin to each other on the water & across
its blue echo
& thinking of horses & houses & now soon after midday there are great ob

-long blotches like a stain
of milk & a great spider spreading itself along the pale glazing bottom of
the water. and this great planet passing upwards towards us
out this silence & drifting & blessing of the water

※ 100m sharks are assassinated each year for their fins – their carcasses thrown back into the sex of the sea – to make
fine Chinese fin soup for you to sit down & dine
w/yr sip spoon & napkin all over the wide open restaurant eye of the world
CNN NewsReport seen in Ja on the friday of arrival there

GUANAHANI

*flying over the Bahamas 12 Oct 1492 on AJ 016 over the US Easter Seaboard of Gauguin
of Afghanistan 11:19am/w/the pilot beaming us the news that the cold front from the North
we are leaving is following us South bringing this kind of history*

(1)

How come
along the East Coast of North America
almost to noon . the thin white line of the long beach

the clouds coming right down on the water like ice-floes
like thousands of tiny floating islands in an ornage tint of water
*what makes me say **Soufrière** at the beginning of the world*

(2)

The midday now xtracts the colour from its genesis
so that there is this dark blue . deep-smoke almost indigo
a total absence of mango . illava of the land

lakes make of mirrors . wriggles of silver rivers
spots spots spots of bright islands in the dead landscape
turning away now from the Atlantic at 11:34 on this Friday October 12

(3)

What makes me call out Sahara
as we turn slowly between heaven
and this dead earth of flat contours
not even an eagle or a hawk . arrow of the air

nothing living until we reach
the Bahamas where it will be light
blue & green . w/the face of the dream
looking up towards us like leaves . like Icarus

from under the scarface of the water
but right now
Sahara of Norfolk Virginia
not even a fish or a whale

or a plum. not even a tree plummetting
upwards & blazing yellow yellow w/sweet scented fruit or a lumberjack

(4)

Now we are back near the ice-floes drifting over the Arctic's infidelity
of plains of baughnaughcloughbaugh milk floating over placid lakes

liqurid on blue

the water is cold here. not frantic at all
but deep . home of the whales i have miss all morning

(5)

We are right over them now
even a pale aurora borealis
a cold freize on the equator

like the filigree of a tamarind leaf
like the white lace made in Old San Juan
but far softer & not staying long w/us at all

(6)

Now we are truly among these white islands
of cloud. bigger now & *shape like domestic bread far off in ovens*
w/ its dough placated in a pale blue pan of time till we are lost
in the maze between the soft rising in the cravasses between the fat Cockpits
moving on thru time for ever & ever to the bent slow bow & ribbon river
of the horizon

until a voice at last intruders
speaking loudly & inxtricably in *'nation'*
telling its Mother not to ashame or look askanancy over her shoulder
because it is *'fe we language'* and we see

not ice-floes anymore. but clouds soon crowding again
strato-cumulus of beginnings of the moon from 39,000 feet of the spacecraft
seen from this heave & verdure of our language @12:07 past noon

(7)

Now we are black into the ice
& the ice-flows . large plateaux & Dogon cliffs. igloos here & there
long lanes between countries like the long valleys between canefields

tho as i say. this is still all white. not green or yellow blooming. no
wind. not even a windmill. flat
white pasture lands running down to the sea. like at Bull Savannah Bar-

badoes. sweet sweep of the land to the sea before the building of houses. no
tourisses yet surfing. not even lobster-pot catchers surfacing
dripping the sheen from their faces. still light years away from the deep

sound. still far away from my mother's poem

but is wonderful how this witness help me to understand okro
how it is formed from unknown but not forgotten African fingers
how it clings to kukoo. to its languages

its little pink ticking pearly seeds. guava. agave. pale purple cactus flowers
blooming once every twenty-five hundred years
thickening the soup creating this round bottom of the yabba & the bolom

(8)
12:28pm

Now we are somewhere over Central Turkey
thinking of the Dardanelles. some musician

whose name I can't remember playin vibes on a 78 I have lost
thinking of Central Asia. Ozzajistan. Tajikstan. Afghanistan. the mos

beautiful cruel landscapes in the world. the most
beautiful starving people. the most

beautiful women veiled in pale blue burkhas of dust . the most
bomb. bombarded . the most

spectacular ruins . rubble like a Beethoven symphony
stigmata

the strings of their voiolence & their one multiple continua
voices. mantras of tabla music. darker

than the Hindu Kush more Arabian more Red Sea more African more Nile
w/out the verdure & the fertile water

and now their bearded warriors. drugged. handcuffed. shaved. blind-
folded over the Caspian over Mt Blanc over the white cell blocks of the Alps

the Atlantic where we are now flying
& be landed at Guantánamo Américano of all places

unplacated in cages
their heads & faces. their full souls & bodies. xpose to the weather. not

even like horses or cattle w/out rights against torture
& the soft hiss of injustice & patience & poultice

(9)
And i realize that i have been thinking of them all morning from this high
freeling air. watching the clouds changing shade into the fate
of their future . into landscape & memory

into the bleak beautiful meaning of reality
plummetting towards my own horse of ruins
& dreams. of how they too will be forgotten in time

as the ice-floes melt back into the cirrus of their mothers their lovers
those who have love them. outer wheels
& limits of spiral galaxies triangeles parachutes. shapes of magenta

stealth bombers ghosts shrouds
Tibetan journeyings spaces of time between magnets & continents
causeways into another continuum. approaching the new life of Eleuthera

(10)
el12:50pm
Lucaya Abacos Andros & now Eleuthera comes into view
coral necklaces writing on the water
cosmograms of fish & the halls of sunken ships
hieroglyphs of the beginnings of blue

and now it begins to get very green
like the first ever light which will be Guanahani. a light
you have nvr seen before. like at the back of yr eye
in its private room

like at the bottom of the ocean beyond sunset & dawn
beyond angels & borealis. come
from the depths of the sea. continent
of dead ice. from the land

of three hours of mirage moving thru space
w/out motion. only the landscape un-
folding like scroll like metaphor. suggesting some-
where Xuma. Samana. Mayaguana. Inagua

decorations of unrequited flesh
green that breathes
life. as if there is wind
at last. because there is wind

(11)

like the beginnings - o odales o adagios - **of islands**
from under the clouds where I write the first poem

its brown warmth now that we recognize them
even from this thunder's distance

still w/out sound. so much hope
now around the heart of lightning that I begin to weep

w/such happiness of familiar landscap
such genius of colour. shape of bay. headland

the dark moors of the mountain
ranges. a door opening in the sky

right down into these new blues & sleeping yellows
greens . like a mother's

embrace like a lover's
enclosure. like schools

of fish migrating towards homeland. into the bright
light of xpectation. birth

of these long roads along the edge of Eleuthera
now sinking into its memory behind us

(12)

and the long cirrus now stretching us there
the dark indigo rim of Sungaro
alongside the birthmark of blue
the whales at last here

white puma. white peace. the humps of these huge breathers
and the clouds like sails like ships like white tractor treads
fast flying forward to Cuba
(01:15pm)

and soon is Jamaica
the crinkle of Bogle of Marcus of Marley of Manley of Cockpits
the great heavy bloom
of the mountains. the anvil awaiting its sunlight. the singing

(01:45 this afternoon)

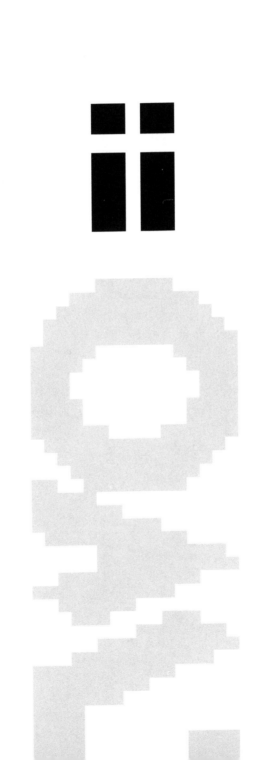
ii

Donna

is escape dem-a farr
musk rose blooms

the tight room w/ its oils. dryin clothes
stale mask of nivea cream

the skin dyin of sweat
the mattrass dryin of rot

she will not open the window for fear of intruders
yesterday the girl rape in the toilet of the carib

cinema by four/fourteen year old yout
yesterday the girl raped comin home from school

yesterday the girl raped in her own home in her own bed
and all her dolours taken

the room stifles the forehead
as the necchi sings

if she had had a child it wd be a girl. sleepin
or a boy suckin his thumb pushin his soles thru a root
in the blanket

you want out de light?

the breasts small and familiar
coconut oil as she stands close
the rayon slip-on thin as skin now

luminous w/ flesh
black span of darkness
your bridge to her world

and she arching growing closer closer
curving as the world curves. as the evenin curves
the wind like a soft fresh of showers

her almond of silence

she enters your soul
displacing your anger the days useless lumber
she lets it xplore

you. converting you prone to columbus
some eyeless african sailor & brings you home hero
circled w/ flowers confetti of love blinding you

but she is lock
still in her island. your key will click
responsive to its prick

of heat

the gear will shift its metal tendons scraping
wheels tearing the gravel as darkness xplodes in the engine. hoot
owls of the light blinkin on at the grate of the gateway

an lard how it hot
how a greasy
an de pickney dress dem to dun

an de long track a night tick tickin tick tickin
machine petal clatterin on
an de clock a de dark stuck at 1.35 1.35 1.35 1.35

see how me eyes cyaan prop open even
an de rent to pay
an anoder one comin tomorrow

an who will remember dem ancient a days
dat a walkin to school. shooters hill walkers wood
ocho rios. how me prangalang down to camperdown town

an de man want i sleep wid im
an i got me xam
an de man seh mek i go wid im

an i can hardly stann to look pan im
but what yu go do when yuh belly gone slack
& yu young jookin gifted an black?

im drive away now
in im company car
in im see-through shirt

in im rolex

while i sittin down here wid dis fine toot comb
tryin to scratch out de lies dat i tell
cause a girl got to learn not to get too ole

nat to let it look dat she belly gone cole
for these men who is here tonight
an tomorrow dem gane. . .

DAYS _ NIGHTS

for Jean Rhys & Tia Wilson

•

- the part of the poem in this performance of the poem is played by Christophine -

•

Days

Um was a likkle black dog
bow leg waggle tail whipper-snapper
wid nuff plenty snuff colour fleas

ann feedin it pap in de kitchen

judge jackson was out
gone for de day dung to pleasant hall
but for all yu know by now he in town out by de churchwall pun
mason hall

street or clickin up sticks in de folly

mistress jackson home doh
an miss speckle-face varney dat doan say a ting
an miss betty .

nine years ole whe de trouble start

evva see a cat dat does rub up it furr
pun yuh foot nice nice nice: soff an purr when um feel
like it?

evva see a cat dat does peel it purr
pun yuh foot when it feel
like it: an den when it done: when it dun rub yuh dung

de chat gone
gone long like if it doan know yu
from adam or even ezeekiel?

betty so

.

nine year ole betty jackson get outta she bed an nine ocock strikin

mistress jackson she mudda is get up at twelve
when de face a de daylight start fight-
in it shadow .

she gettin on now
she nerve shallow
cock-a-doogle crow got to grow
into hee-haw bray a de donkey
fore de wood say flax an yu know she unshatta she shutta

.

but betty up early
an bo
is trouble she shellin

nevva trouble trouble
true
till trouble trouble yu

smood pebble a tongue in she mout an she garglin
all dem holes hatchin outta she mout: she int want dem:
she even beg ann for a chawstick to chew wit

an she brushin she teet an she garglin .
dem learnin .
she get up an nevva say mornin

.

ann sittin down dere in de half open door light
feelin cumfie an cool pun she bottsie
she face part shadow an happy

bird songs touchin de bread crumbs she got in de bucke
dere soakin in milk
de doctor bird visit de hibiscus tree
an de hoverin green of it wing in ann eye

when it move
de light of it brilliant wash up pun de silk
a she skin like shea wata

·

ann feedin de puppy

got it cotch in she lap wid it head in de bucket when *bap*
betty mek one grap at de lil pappy. *so*

an de puppy-head turn rounn an *whelpit*
bett rip back she hann as if he did bite
it an nearly fall ova ann foot pun de floor

she cyaaan help it
she head hit de door an de door
handle rattle an de doctor bird back backin quick quick outa de
flowers an gone

not a sparrowbird song in de t'icket

·

it guh so

bett stann by de door an she rubbin she nobbit
movin she mout like she chewin dry
stick: den leggo one turruble kick
at ann head

me see how she foot bottom dutty

ann sideways she head from de knock
a dat blow an she rock back quick before betty cud know an

drive one butt
in she backside

look me crosses now nuh
look de trouble me see
de two o dem mekkin one big pappyshow

ann quiet an long
yu cud see how she fingers
like splints or like splinters

how she natty head dread
so is ketch ev'ry hook
an eye in de nettle an grass a de hickey

how she neck-stem risin up cool
an vase from she breast-bone
how she shoulder blades balancin quiet an
strait like a brass-scale(s) .

dat she growin up strong

betty wrong

.

she know in she poor-backra heart
dat she wrong . but she got she two hanns up pun she hip
an she mout pout out like a nayga

what a way she learnin me whisper

nine knobble knee years growin up from de grounn an aready she
know how to skiffle an tack wrapple roun in de wind to get what she
wish when she want

it

cyaan beat ann she self
but she self goin get ann a beat-
in . yu

wash

it

.

yu drownin de dawg in de liquor. man ann

do wha? hook back ann
mekkin to gih she a jook wid she elbow

i int got needa dog in no lappit-face pap
an yu know
it

yu bekky-face nigga

ann custom to kick an scratch in dis place
jack johnson goin breed an born from she waise
he goin carry on bad an mash up yu face

.

yu see betty say
yu see what she say?
who yu callin a nigga yu nayga

an she squeeze-up she dry-wata pas'e like a wash-
rag an cryin

.

what a way dem is mek we burn in we black-
ness . what a way dem is trouble me see

maaaa . betty bawl out . she face makin *waaaa*
ann tellin story out bey pun me

she doan feed de dawg . jook she hann in i back
an say dat i faava a nigga

Nights

remembering Tony McNeill

Scratchin she thighs an de sides a she belly
she head stickin outta she nightgown like duppy
mistress jackson open she mout an begin

yu fuhgettin yuself yu lil senseh-head betty
i tell yu aready doan mess wid miss betty

jess heiss dat pappy dawg beck in yu lep
fore i swim yu in licks wid dis catty

hear ann

me feed it aready mish jackson an dun
look how de dog belly fum: it tann tum

·

yu yellin at i, yu saucer face ninny
yu tryin to tell i i doan know de beat of i own pappy

dawg an it mout when it finish an done?
tek it up, mek i tell yu, or i skin yu like skim milk or scum

ann cut she eye baad
like she doan know she place
an she pout out she mout like a nayga

she grab up de poo where it splat pun de floor
but she choopse up she toot like yu mout rippin clot
an de clot was mish jackson face

·

ann only twelve years
if yu look pun de smood at de side a she face
yu cud see

it

down dere in de pool a she neck
watch how dem feinty lines

crossin de cool like a cob-
web an ketchin de light when she stretch-

in

but under she dress
all up an dung she back an she back-
side c'dear, all dung de back a she foot

look how she have to hop pun she side-
step . how
de ankle-bones twiss

how de stock marks lock in she flesh
yu see how she spine?
all dem fine bones chip up an jigg like a grater

look how she knucks flatten
an raff . under she half-rip slip-cotton dress
she skin strike up & down like a razor

she belly & tie all welt-up & silver
like she fright in a i-
ron cage wid a tyger

''

how much am i bid?

nan
nan
nan

anan

nvr a man

nam

i see bugles shields gunmetal un-
glints: guttering eagles
comin to meet me

i hear the coiner's voice of the fat auctioneer
the pulpit his strumpet
& chair

makin meat of god's wonders
her neck the globes of her ear
& her lightning

how much am i bid?

do i hear amber
do i hear blue
do i hear mambo

do i hear yu
four five sex and a live tv
shew

do i jook
do i cook
do i hook

onto yew

flushin yu out with my soap flakes & fire
rustlin yu out with my germ heat
& wire

do i wear
do i wear
do i weary yu down

how weep
how steep can yu hide me
how cryin away

from yr heavy horizon
of fear
how high

will yu bribe
will yu bribe
me

how much am i bid?

nan
nan
nan

anan

nvr a man

nam

fat pappy squeal out when de flicker flack out
an it whimper an weal in ann lap

nan
nan
nan

anan

nvr a nam

gnashlish

•

•

•

Iwa

my mother say i be alone
and when I cry

(she say)

i be columbus of my ships
and sail the garden round the tears that fall into my hand

i cry

but on the seas three nuns appear
black specks stalk the horizon of my fear

sancta marias w/ black silk sails
were these the swift ships sent from harbour?

was this the fleet my pride unfurl?
pirates in smiling ships. they rob the world I rule

and not a trick i bring will bribe their cruel slaughter
for still the black silk walk towards me on the water

i crie

and have not think till now that there is such a bright salvation in a tear
my mudda have not tell me only faith cd sail a sea of glass & fear

have faith to face. caonoba
the tree-green seas roll down

one doubt will smash the garden, shatter the convex lawn. drown
the three nuns of fear

2

See?
she saw

the sea
come

up go down
school-

children summer-
saulting in the park

See?
see

what on the sea
water? some-

thing float-
ing?

See

here are yr bodom
beads . i see

yu take
my chilldren . *bless*

them. mother
teach them yr ways

See?

she see her chill-
dren summer-
saulting in the dark

See?
what on the water?

some-
thing float-

ing

Yu give yr
beads . yu

take my chill-
dren. and now i cannot reach

them. *Christ*
on the Cross. yr cruel laws teach

only to divide
us. and we are lost

w/out yr faith
w/out yr fear
w/out yr tender love

.

See?

i saw
my prayers. lost

bread
float on the dead

water

3

But what good the water
the canefields well started
the wells running over

but our cups broken?

What good the gold
the richest seams carted
the city in clover

but our safes broken

and what good the children
the lemon
girls steadily sweetened by lovers

but their faith broken?

4

And why do the waves come here riding from allotted lands
behind the black barbed wire of rock the white outworks of their foam
why do they come as they do

white hoofs beating high water on sand
leaping our smashed-in wish that they halt that they keep
the boundaries clear?

we wanted land as it should be
hard and firm. the trees deep rooted. the orchards well
spaced. the churches quiet & heavy w/stone

we wish the sea as it shd be
coming & going on the beaches. leaving a line of dried moss &
black sticks at its uttermost reaches

quiet at sundown. restless at noon. land & sea balance by sky
But where are these loud gallopers going. these bright spurs conquering tide & hill

smashing the balance. breaking the scales
the sea-walls down. the promenades taken
the garden the club the merry-go-run

all suddenly fallen & drownnn
the fisherman's boat is broken on the first white inland hills
his tangle nets in a lonely tree. the trapp fish still confuse

after this breach of the sea's balance treaty. how will new maps be draft ed? who will suggest
a new tentative frontier?
how will the sky dawn now?

5

See?

i see
my chilldrens chilldrens chilldrens chilldren summer-
saulting at the bottom of the dark

6

dumb
dumb
dumb

there is no face
no lip
no moon

the tambourine tinkles
the room rumbles
clouded w/ drums

a crack ascends the silence
soles of my feet
are tall

are tall
are tall
the sky is no wall

at all

the messenger spins
she wears white
calico whispers

the smooth silvers
and tears
the water is waiting

dumb
dumb
dumb

in the dumb
room the crack
widens .   the eye

screams

the knuckles knock
it ajar
the door

opens and the wind is near

dumb
dumb
dumb

the drum trembles
the knocking wakes its sound
the tambourine tinkles

and my feet have found the calling
clear the bubble eyes
the river

If this is all
i have
if this is all

i have
i can travel no far
-ther

you must pour
you must pour
you must pour me

out. so the god
can enter the silver
so god can enter the river

yu must spill
me into the crack
(ed) ground

i am blood
i am pebble
root hairs & the dust of the thunder's room

i am water
i am blood
i am the hot rum leaking from green

from the clanking of iron
i bleed w/the fields' sweat w/ the sweet backs of labour
my steps take root in the worn shadows where the noon has burnt a harbour

dumb
dumb
dumb

and my feet have found the calling
clear the bubble
eyes the river

now the drum speaks
flat palms open their lips
give light to the tight

eyes

the tambourine wrinkles
white shrieks as the messenger whirls faster &
faster

If this is all
i have

If this is all

i have
i can travel no farther

you must pour
you must pour
you must pour

me out
so the god can enter the silver
so the god can enter the river

you must spill
me into the crack
(ed)ground

i am blood
i am pebble
root hairs

and the dust of the thunder's room

i am water
i am blood
i am the hot rum leaking from green

from the clanking of iron
i bleed w/the fields' sweet
w/the sweat blacks of labour

my steps take root in the worn shadows
where the noon has brunt
a harbour

dumb
dumb
dumb

now the drum speaks
flat palms open their lips
give light to the tight

eyes

the tambourine wrinkles
white shrieks as the messenger whirls
faster &

faster

lips curl into old shapes
thick gutterals
red heavy consonants furl on the dry tongue

and the god is near

He moves slow-
ly slow-
ly slow-

ly

He moves slow-
ly
the dark swells

mountain
mountain
mountain

near
me

Now I can smell
his sweat
his musk of damp and slave

ships

his heat hurts
me. my
belly is tight. his hands hunt

me into sound

mountain
mountain
mountain

the god moves
the god moves
me

all around me
is light. can you see
me?

Slowly
slowly
slowly

the dumb speaks

But you do not understand

for there is an absence of truth
like a good tooth drawn from the tight
skull. like the wave's tune gone from the ship's hull

there is sand
but no desert where water can learn of its loveliness
volcanoes w/out their living eyes

the streets of my home have their own gods
but we do not see
them. they walk in the dust

but are hidden from our eyes
even tho the knuckles of my friends' knocking
open their secret doors

the orange on the table
the grapefruit. the cashew
nut. these are our votive offerings

but we do not use
them. the limes in the market praise
them. and the green teeth of the chewing herds

their cross is the street that runs down to the harbour
it is cobble w/voices
it shines like the crabs' backs after the rain

the streets' root is in the sea
in the deep
harbours

it is a long way from Guinée

but the gods still have their places
they can walk up out of the sea
into our houses

the street directs them upwards like blind incense
they find their way thru the rusty holes of our shacks' innocence

Every tree praises them
every ambition that aspires

the drum praises them
and the rope that loosens the tongue of the steeple

they speak to us w/the voices of crickets
w/ the shatter of leaves

MMASSACCOURRAAMANN

Sam Selvon & the 9/11 kanaima foresheen in CD's Canada
Cyril Dabydeen, **Stoning the Wind** (Toronto: TSAR 1994), 83+pp

One

Dear Cyril . the (3) books [**Coastland: new & selected poems 1973-1987** (Mosaic 1989) . **Discussing Columbus** (Peepal 1997) . **Stoning the wind** (TSAR 1994)] arr yester day I open them first thing after sunrise

is rightaway i can see that **Stoning** (1994) is OTHER - even the cover *[show the covers]* - that Guyana tho still there[1] - there's a new & nother even nether direction: 'At the bend' '"I am becoming. . .Canada."' 'Gulf War' yr Mother (how her poem ends in wh-

at kind of enigma[2] in what kind of *algoriddim*[3] . really) . yr Grandma - *a transcontinental-*

---

[1] I will see what I must see:
things of other days.
perfections; the spirit too
is bougainvillea
amidst taller trees, shrubs,
rhododendrons,
spiralling like stars. . .
['The Garden and the Glass', p3]

'The Calypsonian', p18, 'Who we are', pp32-33, 'The CIDA poet writes of Guyana', pp25-26

If I am preoccupied with the tropics
let it be: place of birth, mud, soliloquies,
or madness that lies fallow in the brain -
['December is Winter', p65]

[2] My mother tries pronouncing
The name Macdonald as she stares at a monument,
The first Prime Minister. . .I tell her to learn
His name well. . .she will soon become a Canadian citizen.
She smiles, and says when you visit someone
You must always take a present (it's our custom).

She will never receive old-age pension,
Nearly two hundred dollars a month in four years' time;
Recently she returned home to visit her daughter
Who gave birth to a child weighing eleven pounds!
["I am becoming preoccupied with Canada", p74]

[3] see pp56-57

ization my brother - before our eyes . a Caribbean Oronoco poet becoming transform - no - *interform(ed)* by the saskatoon calgarian landscape of the northern amerindi-< ans of yr instinct even tho. on the surface. yr ikons[4] try resist this - SELVON'(s) POEM betraying *(no!) revealing* it all - one of the great TESSTAMENTS of our lit leh-me-tell-yu . even tho there isn't much trace of the physical (to us) *familar* Sam < if-yu-kno-what-i-mean . As soon as one

O

pens this book of surmise . yr *timehri* STUNNINN-WE INTO-THIS-FUTURE ('I watch distant ly with eyes fixed on the past, the present/Browbeating us because of what I long to hear, and will >> not!')[5] and its there. in Sam. as i said. and so so so so so in 'Stoning' *cheesus!* these ghosts you so call out *seven years before the 9/11* that happen here in

New York MMI

Two

Sam's poem (the po about Sam) is a chimera. . a true ghost. U see it & then it's no long-er here and yu-wonder what trick yr vision rees. But it's because it's call 'Cogita-ting' (pp15-16) and only then in different smaller type '*for Sam Selvon (1923-94)*'<

Here at last is one perfectly prepared receptive poet. responding honestly to the in-timate presence (present) of a friend. a compatriot more so than ever in this narrow

---

4 the persistence of Euro (& EuroAm) ikons (& literary icons p47), Russia, 'American styl (e)', Wayne Gretzsky, Van Gogh, the *Chelsea Club, even 'In praise of Royalty'(!)/p41)*

5 'Grandma's Grammar', p27

intimate xile signifayed as in a small sleeping hotel bedroom and a great writer/ person w/all the aurora of a perhaps crucial moment of crisis - glimpse like evva-< ting-else in the remarkable metonymy of yr poem. in like a twilight zone submerge /emerging consciousness 'end-zone' of 'troubled sleep' - not on the podium but >>> haunted & x**hausted** afterwards. the honesties tryin to escape into sleep ('Morpheus') but even then hounded by the lips of like delirium dreaming out of it. the surfaces of word & whisper so very close to revelation. almost it seems on the verge of dis->> closure. disaster. hoping & hopeless of closure. the uttarest moment of xile. what it feels like when we think/feel we're shut off/shut down - one of the most vulnerable & 'meaning' moments we've so very far recorded in the history of Caribbean liter-ature

That night, in Saskatoon, you drinking steadily almost; *[note how the 'almost' sets up the seed of the uncertainty here; itself offset by the cool conversational tide of the verses; first sign/signal of the presence of enigma]*

another Scotch in hand, and thinking about your invitation to me
- resonances being also the words you ply, come to think of it.[6]

At first the mundane focus is on the writing narrator poet (CDhimself). how will he escape the commitment of his love & respect for the perhaps ?ill & older man. And the medium is already sleep, already half-asleep, that deep area of threshold & <<< transitional transXction

After my reading you insist that you will need
to sleep at the hotel, same room as mine.
I immediately cringe because of my not being able
to fulfill a request, which is also like closing one's eyes
to half-wakefulness, or this naturalness of dialect from a far island
with a mountain range trinity-peaked in your vision. . .[7]

---

6 'Cogitating' (hereafter 'Sam'), p15
7 ibid

The nxt stanza begins the entry into Sam's ambiguous territory - the fissure of the xile trapped in the Other landscape, longing for home and yet knowing it almost like chimera like ghost . tho there's the abiding strength for the fight w/for th present. the crisis

> Now in the heart of the prairie, a Calgarian's life
> is all you live by, muttering in your sleep, with half-moans,
> even grunts that betray a shortcoming of Columbus' own...
> This too is telling me, us, about the real instinct
> to ferret out memory - [8]

memory being now the one possible threshold in/to or out/of dilemma -

> though never born of Canada
> but always your own created Moses or Galahad -
> or another book about London's Blacks. Such perseverance
> in the early hours,[9]

the entry now of what I call above *interformation* w/the non-native landscape (notice-to-the-writer). The paradox of the artist's - no matter where - host or resident - commitment to environment. whether sustaining or not. The spirit of the enterprise < falling back on the familiar icon of Columbus *('a shortcoming of Columbus' own')* -

> or the paradox of immigrants
> who have exiled themselves for lack of shame,
> *who betray origins in one long leap*. . .Canada now awake,
> or you will always be lonely. . .[10]

So that in the middle of the night. in the miggle of this vast continent's xile. watch ing the great writer's fitful ?fretful sleep. Dabyd. thru the dreaming medium of << Sam. begins to confront himself - his own fitful fretful guilt that in perforce 'becom ing' Canada (tho is nvr a Q of 'Canadian') he is betrayin Guyana. even ?betrayin ?Mus lim ?Hindu - **the origins in one long leap** - the alternative penalty of

[8] ibid
[9] ibid
[10] ibid

loneliness. and visibilizing this into a 'creole' impalage - *native stele* - BLACK HOLE OF COSMOS that crucially influences these poems - the Pitch Lake at La <<< Brea Trinidad whe the 'static' dilemma is suddenly resolve in this astonishing imagem of *both things at once* - stasis & its opposite - 'moving' the way a ghost - a dupë a < douen - a *mmassaccourraamann* - wd - the xtraordinary syn*napsis* of

> constantly shaped by crossings...
> the pitch-lake at La Brea no less a longer stride
> without your being stuck![11]

which achieves the sense of simultaneous multiple representation[12] that one become(s) aware of on the verge of discovering metaphor or making love or entering spirit possession - leading to this passage of quite remarkable magical realism - all the more impressive because it sustains the same unhurried flattening prosody w/which the poem begins & which it maintains throughout its continuum - the long nigh(t) becooming memory - that's the (postToniMorrison)word CD keeps calling to us - of the MiddlePassage/MiddlePassages . MiddlePassage of history . African/East Indian . MiddlePassages into the Atlantic of the prairies . into the prayers & xpensive xpanses of xile . MiddlePassages of career & tired hopeful talent . Middle Passages of middlelife . two ships crossing each other's meridiam in a living hotel of sleep -

> So when you snored [usually hilarious but is not so here], I stirred - and heard you say, "Awake, man?"
> I called out, as if from afar, with waves at my eyelids,
> further memory really: maybe a captain yet with me, ahoy!
> The reading I did: images like swords still lunging in the dark,
> the sun's shaping weather while yet you stir, again.
> "Was I asleep? snoring?" I mutter a vague reply,
> akin to a cabin's darkness - the hotel's silence all, wavering across a
> littoral, glittering seas really...[13]

---

11 'Sam', pp15-16

12 The very heart of jazz & metaphor is here; the concept most imaginatively xplored by J J Figarola in ***Sobre muertos y dioses*** (Habana 1989) & continues by KB in ***MR*** (2002), pp107-120 & passim

13 'Sam', *p16*

In these conundrum situations. what can we say? There's only home or oasis - both w/their limitation contradictions. But Dabydee here chooses *neitha*. Instead he goes for *osmosis* - the opposite. in fact. of *neitha*

> At two o'clock in the morning, unbearable time, dreadfully asleep
> as you might be - waves lashing no less. . .I too tread [how close
>
> this is to 'tried' & 'tired'] on water,
> never like Christ, only salvaging more of memory
> before your departure the next morning in a plane's sudden
> but determined *ascending!* [14]

Three

At the base of Cyril's interformation - the tropical colonial adjusting to the new << landscape of colder alien metaphor. still clinging to the old colonial ikons. glimp-(s)ing the northernAmerindian alliance. but not yet ready for it. not yet ceritain how to handle it and if handling it makes sense in im own personal/cultural situation. One tends to build from what one knows from what one is comfortable with << what one has inherited - the kind of language we speak - tho as you can see from Selvon poem. there is a trouble tongue insisting on the lips of the sleep of xile . on the tips of the trouble dreams of transition And there's also deep guilt about the wh ole thing. the quarry the quandary the dilemma the - *who knows* - possibility of quag mire - the haunting but liberating memorium of Trinidadian La Brea[14a]

No where better played out [screen] than in the iconography of the basic women of the scene - the Mother and even more powerfully of course. since even closer to the root of time/farther away from the new (also ancient) future of Canada - the Grandma - who is the only avatar of the volume who uses nation-language - a (in this case modified & mediated) NL[15] mediated & modified thru the *plume* of the offspring. to xpress this same sense of unease ?guilt we first glimpse in 'Selvon' -

---

14 ibid ital in txt

14a That poem in fact follows 'Sam' - pp16-17 of **Stoning**

15 Nation-language/see KB, ***History of the Voice*** (London & POS: New Beacon 1984)

Hear wha me a say,
hear me good; praise de lawd
when he go mek you bring out pickney
who one day go want fo become teacha or docta -
if not a lawya

Praise de lawd when you belly start fo buss,
when you han an foot go tremble,
cause is creation-time -
cry-time, pain-time. . .

Leg wide open, patacake open -
an a child does come out
right here in Canada -
dis same one who go speak
Queen's English widout accent

Who go laugh at the side o' he mouth,
who go be soft-spoken,
go be ashamed o' you too
when you eat wid han'
cause you not care 'bout knife an fawk.

He go say you na gat table mannas. . .
dis same child who'll play in snow,
taak bout Wayne Gretzsky like he a one big hero. . . [16]

So that instead of MAN at this triâge - and Dabydeen xplores - indeed confronts - this dilemma - challenge of cosmologies - clearer perhaps than any other xile duppy-conqueror - the first & second stele of interformation - the creolization of the opp-> ress in the oppressor's landguage (tho the concept of *oppressor* can be dis/toroting > here. since the parameters are far more ffluid & subtle in the reality of intercultur-

16 'Belly-Mumma', p28

ation. esp dur periods of nominal 'peace' - tho since 9/11[17] even the concept of peace haffe be demodified politically legally psychologically and in all-sorts of way(s))

Sam leaves the poem ascending determinedly away from the poet's problem in a sil ver plane. But then comes -

four

'Stoning the Wind' where like miraculously - altho Dabydeen has clearly been pre paring himself for this most watchman moment of this all his life till now - we find ourselves in the middle of the conseQuences of dilemma. of still unresolve dilemma - at last the 'real' magical realism of the mmassaccourraamann - this pressage/presage of the perhaps first major countercatastrophe of our 'modern' (modem . Westem) temne/time - the Middle-Passage-conseQuences in what is now call < 9/11>

> It is a betrayal,
> hibiscus,
> red-red -
>
> The village
> close to the river,
> the high bridge,
>
> The world's really;
> a Muslim in you,
> father -

---

[17] The morning of 11 September 2001 when two hijacked passenger airliners were flown like torpedoes into the Twin Towers (MARASSA) of the World Trade Center complex in Manhattan - the tallest, most 'visually valu- able' landmarks of the City, resulting in the loss of +3000 human lives and untold other animal & vegetable spirits in one single holocaust and event - the first time that this Atlantic metropole is successfully attacked & symbolically & deVASTatingly on its ikons & therefore on its very cosmological equilibrium

Non-believer -
you who stood aloof,
a sharp knife

In your hand,
tearing at the silhouette
of the wind -

My mother
collapsing
on ruinous ground.

Waves of the sea,
all the tides'
undoing -

My forehead throbbing;
this fury
of a long night -

Lunging at the woman
in white -
an apparition

You say -
the moon coming down,
slowly.

Tremor of hands,
and knees,
clods of earth -

The village making
amends, mother,
you pedalling -

Or pining
at the sewing machine,
one stitch at a time

Redeeming us -
with more than
cloth's whiteness

> Made brighter,
> or raised higher
> in the dark.[18]

Five
Dabby's Response

The 'sunrise' of #One is my response
to the receipt of Dabby's books esp
as you see Stoning the Wind. I'm curious that
he didn't reply rightaway & wonder
if what I am so positively & enthusiastic-
ally saying has upset the authar -
was i being perhaps too enthusiass. tic?
Eventually arr a series of apologies -
travel, computer breakdown,
the usual writers' creativity
and then inter alia the wonderfully this -

---

[18] 'Stoning the Wind', pp30-31

25 feb 02

Hello Kamau

My grateful thanks for your note on receiving the books,
and more particularly for your observation on the "trans" thing occurring,
changing me, tho as I write
this--it's an odd thing--I feel I am still the same guy
: the past, where I came from, the identities, India, Africa, Europe, the Americas,
in all of us, the "extra-terroritorial", even the "multilingual matrix"

. . moving around cultures, not just one homeland," and so on (George Steiner).
If Sam Selvon were around, I imagine us all having a nice chat about this.
Sam used to come to my home for drinks/food whenever he happened to be
in Ottawa.

I like Wole Soyinka's idea too: "I am [a] writer and therefore an explorer.
My immediate tribe remains the tribe of explorers."

(I smile; I just write, and don't dwell on these things as I write.
Let the writing take me along, somewhere, or everywhere.)

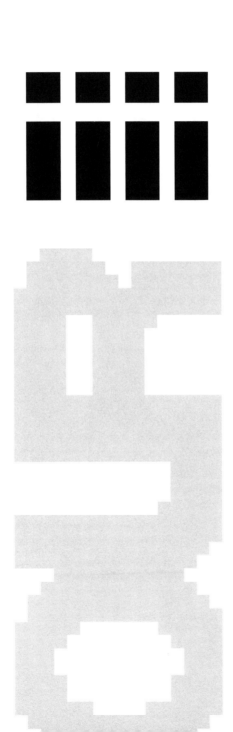

>[]I WAS WASH-WAY IN BLOOD[]<

The Barbados Advocate, Thursday, January 19, 1995, page 4

MILDRED COLLYMORE told the No.3 Supreme Court yesterday that when she recovered from an attack with a stone > she found herself "washed-way" in bloo (d).

Collymore said also that accused Philamena Hinds came back to move the >> rock but she would not let her.

The complainant said that on the day of the incident she left her home and went over to her daughter's on the other side of the road to cut the grass from around the place. When she got to the spot she said dirt was on the grass and she took the hoe and raked it away.

While she was doing this, the witness < said, Hinds' son, Gline, came and spoke to her and then went back up the road. Sh (e) said Hinds came next and spoke to > her but she did not hear what she said.

The witness added that she was holdin (g) down, and on looking up she was >> struck suddenly with a big rock in her right forehead.

"I tumble down and when I come to myself I was wash-way in blood," she testified. . .

Collymore told the court [that] after she found out she was bleeding she went to a neighbour's home and called the police.

She was later taken to the Queen Elizabeth Hospital and detained for three << days, she said

Asked by prosecutor Ms Donna Babb if she had quarrelled with Collymore be-> fore the incident she replied no. The witness also told the prosecutor that >> she did not interfere with the accused.

Babb asked her if she had attacked the accused with a hoe but she said she >> was not given a chance to do so.

Cross-examine

When defence lawyer Dr Waldo Waldro-(n) Ramsay's turn came to cross-examin (e) Collymore, he asked her how long << she knew the accused and she said it < was since childhood. She also said she and Hinds once worked together and th ey understand each other.

Waldron-Ramsay suggested to the wit-< ness that on the day of the incident, <<< marl was on the accused woman's property and she was pulling it down to <<< make a road for her daughter and son-< in-law.

She denied the suggestion.

He further told Hinds that she told the < accused that she could not stop her fro-(m) pulling down the marl, and this she denied.

Waldron-Ramsay put it to the witness th at when she refused to stop moving the marl the accused left her and went bac-(k) home, but Hinds said this was not < true.

Continuing his cross-examination, Wal-dron-Ramsay suggested to Hinds that < Collymore came to her a second time an (d) told her to stop raking away her dirt but the witness [the accused!] again de-nied this ever took place.

The witness further denied the suggest-ion that this second time she became << more vicious and told the accused [Hin-ds] that if she did not move her

"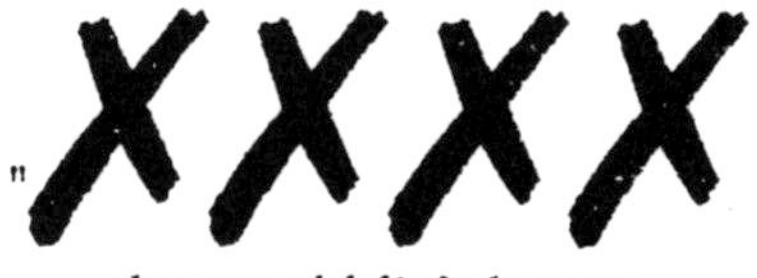

she would lick her to

down."

Waldron-Ramsay also suggested to Coll ymore that she had the hoe in the air >> ready to lick down Hinds, but she den-ied this.

DATE TREE HILL CASE

The Crown will call its third witness this morning in the trial of 48-year-old Philamena Hinds, before Mr Justice Frederick Waterman in No. 3 Supreme Court.

Hinds, a machine operator, of Date Tree Hill, St Peter, is charged with causing griev-ous bodily harm to 65-year-old Mildred Collymore, of Date Tree Hill, on December 13, 1993, with intent to maim, disfigure or disable her. . .

Hinds, who pleaded not guilty. . .is represented by attorney-at-law Dr. Waldo Waldron Ramsay while the Crown's case is being put by Acting Crown Counsel Donna Babb.

Collymore's 45-year-old daughter, Linda, is acting as her interpreter, because the wit-> ness has a hearing problem.

Bread

Slowly the white dream wrestle(s) to life
hands shaping the salt and the foreign cornfields
the cold flesh kneaded by fingers
is ready for the charcoal for the black wife

of heat the years of green sleeping in the volcano .
the dream becomes tougher. settling into its shape
like a bullfrog. suns rise and electrons
touch it. walls melt into brown. moving to crisp and crackle

breathing edge of the knife of the oven .
noise of the shop. noise of the farmer. market .
on this slab of lord. on this table w/ its oil-skin cloth
on this altar of the bone. this scarifice

of isaac. warm dead. warm merchandise. more than worn merchandise
life
itself. the dream of the soil itself
flesh of the god you break. peace to your lips. strife

of the multitudes who howl all day for ijs saviour
who need its crumbs as fish. flickering through their green element
need a wide glassy wisdom
to keep their groans alive

and this loaf here. life
now halted. more and more water add-
itive. the dream less clear. the soil more distant
its prayer of table. bless of lips. more hard to reach w/ penn-

ies. the knife
that should have cut it. the hands that should have broken open its victory
of crusts at your throat. balaam watching w/ red leak
-ing eyes. the rats

finding only this young empty husk
sharp-
ening their ratchets. your wife
going out on the streets. searching searching

her feet tapping. the lights of the motor-
cars watching watching round-
ing the shape of her girdle. her back naked

rolled into night into night w/out morning
rolled into dead into dead w/out vision
rolled into life into life w/out dream

For the land has lost the memory of the most secret places

we see the moon but cannot remember its meaning
a dark skin is a chain but it cannot recall the name

of its tribe. There are no chiefs in the village

the gods have been forgotten or hidden
a prayer poured on the ground w/water

w/rum. will not bid them come

back. Creation has burn to a spider
it peeps over the hills with the sunrise
but prefers to spin webs in the trees

the sea is a divider. It is not a life-giver
time's river. The islands are the hump-

backs of mountains. green turtles

that cannot find their way. Volcanoes
are voiceless. They have shut their red eyes

to the weather. The sun that was once a doom of gold
to the Arawaks. is now a flat boom in the sky

DEAR PM

dem fine two dead fish
lay out in the plate of his white tongue
w/out language

all their bubbles have gone
all their syllables of living colour & career thru the water
all dis gone

white scales on a white beach
vivid w/sunlight & the time of the v/young playing in the flashing
water . chip

pink pebble shells from the vast kaleidoscope-
ic shelves of the underwater continent. its floor the slope-
ing reef where we walk

magenta of sunlight in the wave & reflected in the magic of yr skin
all in the blue space before the drought in the mirror
before the time when they haul my very skull up here

on this promontory where we keep looking out for
whales fuming passim soffly their white distant trails
like great steamers of premonition

but there are no pearls
of eyes in prospero plantation since this new time begin
since sin

since the clutter of clocks
since the shipwreck
since the beginning of this wound & absence

since all these brown tears of the ocean strewling the beaches sibilence
since this new speechless. this sleepless
since these unspeakable silences
since these black rocks walking on the water

an we wants to kno wha yu make of all this
prime Minister
wha yu make of the bread

wha yu make of all the dead
loaves & fishes on the road. all these poor oomen w/their loads of debt & pain
dark nightly nightingales & unsupportable magdalenes

de mule dem lockin dem womb up bust wid crick crack crack cocaine
in all de clattering prisons of the world
de yout dem wid dem mandolins

by the sea-suck sea-slack sea-sick shore
lingering awhile while the waves smell sweet
and that one w/ the knife in his heart who calls himself Cruel

. shatters the gleamin glass of his face of the sea
because he doan even kno how to smile
because he doan want to smile since he kill the life off im frenn

when he wasn't yet fifteen years ole. im veins singin a new blues strain
a dub version of Apocalypse Now. apopolectic calypso
pM

all the boats of our hopes collapsin in Green Bay in Oistins Tn Harbour
stonin we down dead outside the supermarket at Carlton. upside Stony Hill
the sunlight bearing all these mourners into the dust. the chilldren w/balloons

for bellies blue e3 green e3 bursting yellow at Xmas
why
is this hot bell ringing

in the belfrys of my brothers whe the hoast of yr votes gone
mR Prime Minister
why you cahn feed the poor as you promise . why yu mek we have to rhyme ocean

e3 speech
e3 silences in these dread midnight poems. why all this look like sinnin in de lann
why

all dis salt dat i walkin like my dread cruel brother by the sea
why
do my wife have to sweep all these tears for such a mostrous portion of injustice

when she get rob by de robbers when she get rob by de merchants when she get rob
by yu
Mr Minister of Social Transformation

of the very dress
she wearin of she dignity. havin to beg for a lil bowl a soup an a slice a dry bread
that catchin de weeblesof hard-brain rice e3 social infes

-tation. why
when she only sun in de world get lick-down at midnight & dead
under de rich silver wheels of a smaddy whose fadda-man can give you a call

mR Prime Minister

so that the police doan even bother check dis case. de body leff they in de road
fe people passin tief-off evvating im ave
all e money gone. e leatha belt. even to de two shoe pun im foot

mR Justice Minister

an dis happenin day
in day
out

& no
body shoutin out bout
it

misterMin
-ista & no peace & no patience
because there isnt no justice

dear pM
no juice nor no justice
misterMin

-ista
an yu kno dat picture of-yu dat dem pace-up pun all-a de money dat int wurt a bline
cent not even a bitt nor a pen
-ny dese days?

an uh hear ∂em is wipin ∂em back
-site all ova yu face
in ∂e jeerin jails of fear

& abuse. in fac ∂em wipin all-ova ∂e place
mR pM
an how even ∂en yu ∂oan care

mR pM

cause yu big ∂em say & yu gut get fat & yu at lease
yu smell strong an ∂ah face cyaan even tek notice a one likkle wrong far less
big-wunns

∂ah shit-up & shut-up brown face nevva notice how my same wife who cyyan fine no
help not even a echo
stannin up there by yu corner. rounn the hedge near yu great-house wi∂ ∂e white

rail-up lawn & yu own
shine-eye woman nxt to yu in ∂e new shiney Govvament Rolla
-∂ex limmo. wavin & runnin ∂e wet re∂ lips an she bottom-mout

∂oin ∂e limbo & choosin she smile like if she-nee∂a ∂oan kno
wha happenin ∂own
hey so - two bir∂s of a fair two bir∂s of a featha

she back more nake∂ ∂an when she ∂i∂ born
yu own people sellin we liver fe corn
- & wunna kickin up ∂uss

all over me poor grievin wife . an int notice ∂e knife
in ∂e palm a she hann
mR pM

even while th sirens come
on & de frights a yu motacrade blinkin & blink
-in. an makin de day look like a funny night

.

say wha?

.

like johnbelly guts dop. in down de well

•

tink yu in heaven • but yu livin in h. ell
tink yu in heaven but yu livin in hell

•

V

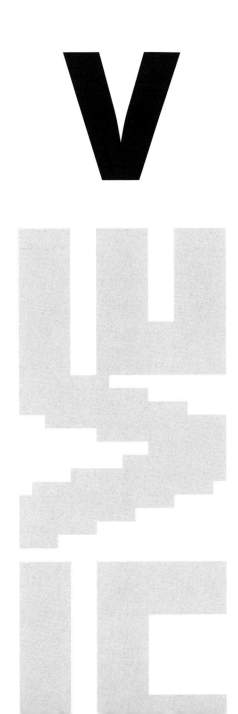

kUMINA

for DreamChad on the death of her sun Mark - mark this word mark this place + tyme - at Papine Kingston Jamaica - age 29
midnight 28/29 April 2001-1002-0210-0120-0020-0000
rev 29 feb 04

WHAT CAN i SAY BUT THIS MY DARLING
WHAT CAN i DO BUT TRY TO SPEECH MY HEART YR HEART FROM BREAKING

•

'Kumina is the most African of the [cultural expressions] to be found in Jamaica, with negligible European or Christian influence. Linguistic evidence cites the Kongo as a specific ethnic source for the 'language' and possibly the music of kumina. There are varying theories as to whether it was brought with late African [arrivants] after Emancipation, or whether it was rooted in Jamaica from the 18th century, and deepened by. . . later Af-< rican influence.

'[Kumina] is to be found primarily in St Thomas and Portland and to a lesser extent in St Mary, St Catherine and Kingston. Kumina ceremonies are usually associated with wakes, entombments or memorial services but can be performed for a whole range of human experiences (births, thanksgiving, invocations for good [or] evil).

'Kumina sessions [*some extending, as in this poem, to* *twenty-one days*], involve singing, dancing and drumming and are of two general types; bailo the more public and less sacred form of kumina, at which time songs are sung << mainly in Jamaican [NL/nation-language]; and country - the more African, and serious form, and at which time *possession* usually occurs.

'Male and female leaders must exhibit great. . .strength in their control of zombies [zambies] or spirits and assume their positions of leadership after careful training in the feeding habits, ritual procedures, dances, rhythms, and songs of a variety of spirits, by a previous King or 'Captain'. . .Queen or 'Mother'.

'One is said to 'catch' *myal* when possessed by one of the three classes of Gods - sky, earth-bound, and ancestral [zambies], these last being the most common form of possession. Each god can be recognized by the initiated by the particular dance style exhibited by the possessed, and by songs and drum rhythms [*bandu, plain cyas, scrap- ers, gourds, tin-can rattles, catta sticks & bamboo stamping tubes*] to which it responds.

'At *bailo* dances, the spirits who are called, more often than not make their presence known by 'mounting' (i.e possessing) a dancer; whose given dance style helps in identifying the spirit, but can span all possibilities of movement. The basic dance posture constitutes an almost erect back and propelling actions of the hips as the feet inch along the ground. The dancers move in a circular [anti-clockwise] pattern around the musicians and centre pole, either singly or with a partner. The arms, shoulders, rib-cage and hips are employed, offering the dancers ample opportunity for variations and interpretations of the counter-beats or polyrhythms. Spins, dips, and 'breaks' on the last beat are common dance variations.

'The journey of the spirits from the ethereal to the mundane world is no less ritualised than other kumina elements. Once invoked by music and other ritual paraphernalia (rum with blood, candles, leaves) the spirits are said to hover near the dancing booth [bood]. If successfully enticed they travel down the centre pole into the ground, then through the open end of the drum to the head of the drum, where the drummer and Queen must < salute its presence. The spirit then re-enters the ground, from where it will travel up the feet of the person sel-< ected to be possessed, along the whole length of the body, culminating with full myal possession in the head of < the [transforming] individual.' Anon, *Jamaica Journal* 10: 1 (Kingston 1986) pp6,7]

•

First it is the knife
in the kitchen. the thick one w/the long bright blade
and the thick wooden handle. that knife wdn't stay
flat. each time i wash it. put it down. it drop or ramp up
on it spine w/the singing edge of the blade running thin
& straight-along like some spiteful future & horizon

Pull out the drawer w/the silvers and it still there. sharp .
prop-over & unquiet on it omen

•

The cosmology of sudden unXpecting disaster
& its unutterable grief unvomiting the world

i seem to be becoming lightning rod
for like this wreck of Time

we cope so tentative so desperate in dis kingdom
of the dread. the voices reach-
ing out. be-
traying fear & crying out for help beyonn the lyme

of reassurance. tryin to mek sense
of all de wallawallawalla as the whole
world like it topple-over menance . tryin
to regain it recompense of balm & balance hallow

>

ello! . . .ello!. . . Mummy!. . . This is Ingriid. . .

Kamau & DreamChad coil in each others blood. she
tieing the discomfort his tears for her dead son
while she bleeds as her sun keels from its mangle wheel .

hit off his latenight midnight bi-
cycle middlepassage ship

by a rat-racing-on-our-highways new-money quick-monkey
ill-legal-jjugs-money-traffikin cyaar -
BMW Audi the sleek black latest luxury Discord or Ellectra
or streak Ajax Mardza or Alexandria - in Papine -

Errol Hill beggarmanpoem . Slade Hopkinson & Breeze
madwoman poems

Ogou. Soyinka. Dennis Scott's Dog. Tony McNeill's Ungod. Vera Bell's Gog -

they happen all here -
the unceremonial graveyard. thirsty & unappease -
of yout. artists. don gorgons. Caribbean

slaves. eee-
lectric politricks & politricans. big big-time robber
baroms

•

the 21 days

on the first day
of yr death it is quiet it is dormant like a doormat
no one-foot touch its welcome. its dust on the floor
is not disturb nor are the sleeping spirits of this house

i sit here in this chair trying to unravel Time so that it wouldn't happen twine

on the second day
of yr death. i break a small

bread

i can still smell the sweet flour of yr firstborn flesh

on the third day
of yr death. the water in my urine turn to blood
i cover the waterfront of the mirror w/a blue cloth where yr face stood

on the fourth day
yu shd be rising. knocking at the door of darkness. coming back to me

i do not hear yr call

on the fifth day
after yr death. a young white rooster. white white white feathery & shining tail & tall
neigbour of sound from miles away in the next village
stands in the yard & from his red crown crows & crows & will not go away

he struts round to the back-a-wall
his one eye clicking clicking as he crows

comes to the glissen of my window & he crows
loud like the overflowing voice of my Trelawny waterfall

on the sixth day

after yr death. there is this silence of flowers
their petals say their shining needs
soft water needs

sweet showers needs
sweet rain from heaven

•

i see them once again inside the chapel of my funeral

on the seventh day

after yr death. the yellow flour
in the cup-cakes in the kitchen have gone sour

there is an eye of rancid in the middle of their meal

i am unhappy like the wind & tides are restless rivers
i can't find you. i can't find you. i cannot cannot cannot be console to dreams

the mad dogs of the pasture kill the cock & pillage
it. madwoman wind is scattering white screaming feathers' petals' pedals over all
the brunt & burnin ochre-colour land

on the eiate day

after yr death
me do nothin. nothin. nothin . i cdn't even get yr inglish 'eighth' spelt streight

on the nine/ff night
yu rise again from off the dead

•

i see you now & at the hour of yr o not soff not soffly dead

it is my pain it is my privilege . it is my own torn flesh torn fresh
o let me comfort us my chile . is not yr heart is broken

on this tenth day
i haffe go down to the Station today to find out
what they doin about yr det. about the 'accident'
dem call it. bout the black-hearted man who a-kill

yu. an whe dem hide yu body
the po. lice who dealin w/ this case they cannot look me in the lips
and No One kno

whe the boy is or gone or when he will come-back
ten time dis ten dem mek me up & down & hook & fourt
to fine my sun. an ten ten time dem ave no ansa for me for me for me

in dis dry-weatha tunda
dem seh because i poor & have no hook to haul-out who
inside dis station. an i inn got no song

to sing becau i colour in dis Marcus Garvey country proud an strong
an wrong - yu sun gone out & still yu colour wrong.
inn got no i say song

i wonda whe Port Royal *is. when de eart goin again goin crack*

my daughta Ingriid walk beside me hurt
an strong an dress in black
her face inside she face int mekkin sport

on the tenth night after a long long distance silence

i born into this world w/nothing but my breath & my bare back an hornets
in my chess

now i will haffe doubt if god is good & black & honesty
wha good god do fe me?
whe god dat cricket midnight criminal when Mark of god get call like dat & kill
Mark cyaan dead so if good. if god

my breath give birt to good like god
my sun dis gold is all my riches that cannot be replace
an suddenly me cannot fine him in dis place before dis good god face to face
wha good fe god. no god. wha good. wha god. no god
if good Mark have no face to face dis god inside dis good god place

on the eleventh day after he dead
[Silence]

on the twelfth day
after yr debt - o pickney - it is as if me cyaaan wake up
Time has been drain from all my clocks. the sky is overcyas & lock
altho it isn't rainin yet

[Silence]

this night we hold our wake. watch w/ the spirit of my sum before his daily funeral
. people cook food bring bread & drink & there's some singing
of the old traditions by the older folks & country citizens

but they soon fall to arguing and they soon fall down to quarrellin
about the words the phrases time & tempo of these sookey tunes
it seem they isolated in the old traditions in these coffee hills

We are 3000 feet high up in the blue mountains of this Irish Town

by three o'clock is gettin cold here in the midnight dew
and all around me. even the young-ones
watch me watch the faces of their coffin spirits growin old

on the tired tireen(th) day
after im det. we tek the body of my son
& walk him from the chapel back up the hill-road
pass Mass Dixon Lane to Bedward buryingrounn & seal him up & tomb
im leave im dere

my aunt husbann tell me later dat tree
time Mark try fe mek dem put im down. de casket get so heavy
de man-dem haffe change sides all de time to ress dem hands
& many willin new ones haffe come fe help dem wid it
im get so heavy heavy goin to im grave

tree
time he try fe stagger dem go left. teach
dem to veer down MasonDixonLane whe e grow up

is all too sudden. Sonny. im want to ress a while from all dis pain an distrulation
cause when im reach down-dey . im nevva soon-come-back again

mi look back once onto the leaf. less barrem hillside where he is
cyaaan even see no grief
of flowers there

•

perhaps there are no flowers there

on the fourteenth day after Mark gone. on the first day after him first entomb
the rain staat fat rat raat . i stannin by the window like a widow washin it

An do you know that even as he lie there in the street
that midnight widdout light. skull crack. neck broken. trauma. red red red
de passerby-dem Marley sing about -
de woman son shoot down into the street & dead ? -

dem tief-off evva thing they fine pun Mark
So when he went down to the policestation morgue that night
my son mange up widdout im shoes & shocks?

on the fourteenth day after my sun gone. on the first day after him first entomb
i feel my womb
seal-up. de blood brek-down inside me bellybottom

[day 15]
i wonder wha appen to im bicycle? i wonder whe um is?

[day 16]
we know 'widow ' an i hear of 'widower'
i wonder what dem call a woman lose she sun?

tief too dat too me reckon

again i sit here in this chair trying to unravel Time
so that it wouldn't happen

[day 17]
Death keep gettin-away & gettin-away & gettin in the way
coilin inside dis house like serpent(s)
into its dark corners when we turn to face

dem
eatin away the cupboards of our soul
above the stove an thru the drains an down in. to the cellar w/its term

-ites. torm
-ites tunnel & un. dermine the very grounn we walk
on. how we make love. destroye the very irie way we dance

they was nvr a chance really that we wd avoid
this. clingin to each others bodies. holdin hands. and climb
-in to our souls. feelin the grief like an electric wire

shudder thru our clothes around our ribs where Adam make
us. veins
our gutteries. our lonely bones

this
we have nvr plan
to be away from love like this

opening these doors one after one one after one
sweeping this dust these ashes from the floor of sorrow
bowed head. the one step one step sweeping

out today today
and down the passage of tomorrow & tomorrow & tomorrow
into the distance of what must be the future but no more no more

each time i turn into the kitchen. head down towards the sink
of chores. lookin a spoon fe wash. fe tea to brew. fe soup to scoup
fe bread fe fat & fry.   is you is you is you. keep

comin back. cockroaches of these curses
flickerin up the pipes & plumbin . lickerin the wet surfaces
w/ they lean

thumb
-nail tongue . the lard
oil ori

-faces washin back yr
face. these grey green oil
-(y)fissures that yu cannot clean

as if we cover up in soares e3 sin. as if we do some
-body some
-thin wrong . as if we do some. body

in e3 spit out syllables like the split
stringy ends of bonavista peas spit
out the white bright taste of salt into this dry lagoon as if this is the saviour

this the recompence. this is the penalty we play for 'coming from no
whe' for 'being poor'
the rat patrol keep rattin pass my door

and now there is this white night blind
-ness in my eyes for all the years
that are no tears to tell. because there are no years no no more years

fe yell for you in this - this - 'new emergency'
— the blood my heart
the broken body wringing in my belly like a ghost my baby like a bell

of bone
. mi wunda whe e doin now
. mi wunda whe Mark gone

[day 18]

Sometime in the miggle of the morn-‹
in of the night i remember that this
day is the day when my urban barn
some undread toussann years ago ‹‹‹‹
an as the custom/as the kind. ness is.
yu muss xpec re. spec. the day shd be
acknowledge/celebrated/be re. mem
bered. don't? But in the miggle of this
grief. all this slow daze of grease. th-
ese sleep. less nights. this fear now e-
very sound each startle shadow nigh
(t) it might be him/my love impale ‹‹‹‹
w/in his pain impassion wounds - *why me*
why me. wha mek me fraid & frighten ee? - **all I cd do is walk**
across the moon an kiss-im pun im
broken cheek my eyes elsewhe & ›››››
hissin not for him today. mi like me
cyaan help whe me travellin-mi-trav-
ellin an wish im Appy Birtday‹

on the nineteen day afta my husbann gone
- it seem so long it seem
mi fatha now altho I nvr kno no fatha
- my husbann gone back

to the States to finish up im work
- few nights ago he try to touch me. wake me up. yu know
as if dat comfort? dat wd help

. . .

ah well. . .he had his 10 years time of salt already an he went thru hell
and now he marréd me the poor man like he have to wear my bell
he nevva try to rush me. dough. . .e mean me mean me well

. . .

on the twentieff day after ee tief and the seventh after de burial
i go lookin for my sun in all his glory
Somethin inside my shake & rackkle heart. along my ripple spine

agroin/agroan my nipple guts. w/in the bleedin womb whe he did born
whe he intomb

something inside here tell me there will be no rest no rest no rest no rest no rest no rest
- can be no rest - until I find him - these rock dry-rivva courses - an bring im justice back
w/me

in true
becau im nvva born to blue nor no slow horses

21

SpaceTime stann still As still as if it didn't happen Tho it is 21 days now & she Nkuuyu is still travellin still travellin in the underworld To find her sun & bring him back kalunga on this earth. That's where she is That's why she is so far away That's why you know she can't leave Kingston at this time to go back w/her husbann to the U nighted States Valhalla & the kingdooms of this world whe they in love might live who knows for. ever For she must find him She will find him They will talk Might take a long long time. but she will come to understand if she can find him find him find him She will accept Perhaps Because she see him like alive again Whole Fit &Beautiful again and he will find her eyes & call her Name again – Beverley Miss Mama Bev Miss Bev And she at last begins to Terrible & bleedin troubleous in pain Such blessèd water after such long drought & shining silence after such long doubt And call him back im name &call him Mark again & Light &Love & take him back & born him - ***O Mama - Mark - O Mama*** *- This xchanging is the healing nor ever healing But she try He try.* ***Name on Name on Mama. Mark on Mark.*** *So she can hold him now w/in her arms again Protect that neck that nor shd be broken. That head that nor shd be crush. so Hush she will rock him Hush she will rock him to sleep And it is almost over*

Now she will try to bring him back
back to the world up
-inside down. down inside black
to the world they have lost of the sun
-light & 'real' Rock
in her cradle of arms of all she can give
to the world. beyond all these harms
& their fissures & failures Sleeping
for all the ages

is when they almost there — door corridor crossroad gateway threshold — the light becoming stronger — less stranger less stranger - almost sounds almost taking shape. the street. the trees. a building. stone. a chirping bird. turtledoves of green. . . That he awake into this his second sudden terror His visor of this otherWorld. mask off. the new face on. eras from like beginning coming to this end. Skull of his breath. Wind colouring itself the long way wrong way wrong way wrong way wrong. the soundless horror of his wounds like the wild white of my eyes first seeing it. then something in side in. side me going red & swimming i in black. the uttar lamentation of this broken blank Look he transforms before her by the doorway into broken fish & pisces. torn from his roots & gender. into this common sound. from all he almost is into what suddenly can nor be. this stripp & vivid unconstructed verb. constricted. In all his cinnamon & dis. assemble parts. His black crown crush. recrush. Th (e) vase neck break. rebroeken. The cruel eye of his assassin in trauma in his lockets

Jeesus my Revelator *Injustice as e dead bit from behine to this afflictuated future. an nor even kno it. Each bless of him the salted water i now drink. His white flesh broken to th-is flesh my red i cannot eat* **No No No No in carne criminate I do not want to see it!**

there is a howling she can hear she does not understand is here is hers. like she is hearing in her own ears howling wolf long canine knives & clanking richter rachets Like all his blood is floating down her cistern of his wounds are blessèd rain this sound w/in her falling

ears this taste w/in her mouth like she is givin birth to menance memory — his past some-how his tirelesslessness & somehow now — his future so me. where in this past where they are bound in what is almost sound in what is almost light & outline — w/in the shadows near the door where they shd pass so they might live — together — as it was before — as it will be. be. fore - is what the sound is saying - giving birth to light — her sun - her son - her cinema - the death that is in him is him becoming death that was-in-him was him. un. coming him - the death that will be him becoming bourne & being born now in this nommonation of these howls so near the 'real' & stranger raiding world now gettin louder gettin clearer gettin war-mer so blinding her now so she can't see him anymore tho she still has the howling in her — and somewhere deep inside her bowels now the sleepin rock. im cradle her familiar spirit arms — the womb of his death now safely wounded in her - sun become father - genitor - an almost newborn born & burn. ing in her - one in one & so always w/in him w/in her in her - learning himself again to live w/in in her wounds

So that at last possibl - even if unbearable to bear - but bearing - still bearing - and at least & at last no(w) possibl - what yesterday was impossibl - a pathway not possibl - no(w) possibl - she leaving him new at this door at this threshold this light of forever w/in her. bearing down

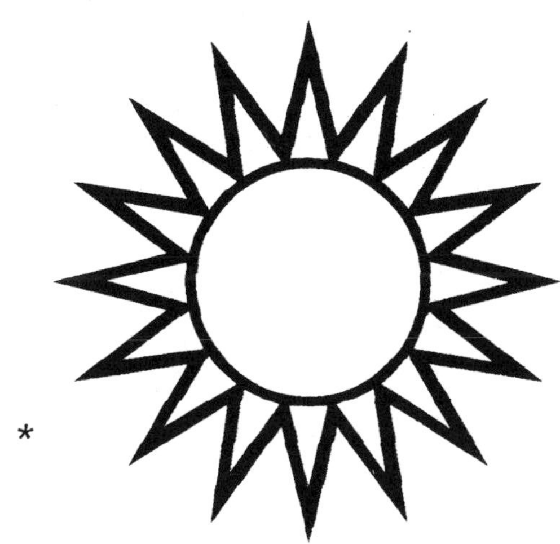

When she return to Irish Town later that night
all the flambeaux are blowin in her house
and they still singin the old Sankey song about Light

- 'They is a light/they is a light/shinin in this house/They is a light/
they is a light/burnin for me now/they is like a Spirit
movin in these walls' -

And as she look up thru the Valley
of Pharaoh Sanders' Sunship where she cd see
the house clearly in the clearing of the turn-
ing road

She kno she wasn't goin back down to August
Tn nor up into Stony Hill or any of these
Kingstone palaces

But back back into whe she born . into the hills
of beginning again of Trelawny home again before
she will able to go-on again . UlsterSpring Healing

& Zion & Byall Thistle SweetBottom OleGermanTown
into Maroon Town & the Accompong of the voices

verri verri a Pongó

as if the sankey itself is the sun
of her tree & the whole sankey tree is singin in the fire

Ooo Mudder Margret
gba kongó yerri
yerri kongó

rikkita rikkita
kongó yerri
yerri kongó

wata woyula wa nkwenda
kongó yerri
yerri kongó

wo ovili m'mwon'
kongó yerri
yerri kongó

wo ovili m'mwon'
kongó yerri
yerri kongó

ye m'merrima
gba kongó yerri
yerri kôngo

9/11

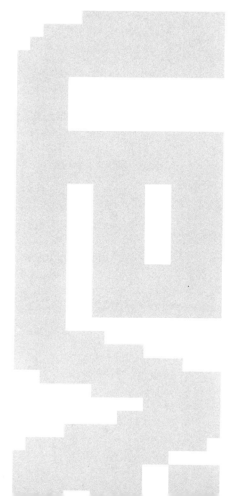

HAWK[]S LAST BODY_SOUL @RONNIE SCOTT[]S IN LONDON 11 SEPT 1967 _ COUNTING

Hawk

shrouded in mirrors. showers. haunted by twins
the waiting windows of the world . voices of falling wires. crumbl
-ing towers long before his time here flare. ing future

Rollins Bridge is fallin down

in london . where he arrives
this spinn
-ing golden time

early like this. this early tinder autumn season
the fly. ing spirits white as snow
-fall falling sorrow

in the chill

embracing tender air that cannot hold
you up *no*
warm canoe my sunûgal

that cannot hold . that cannot hold
you *o my love* my fall
-ing failing fading

leaves o love/o you this golden time in lon
-don early autumn of the first spill
-ing burn

-ing time. the slide
-walks & the chestnut trees. and turn
the last crush corner into Ronnie Scott's

the lights down low already even at the bar
the crowded peering room w/waiters moving in a hush
that eve. ning all these years

a sound I nvr see(n)
till now . walk on the stage to tremulous applause
of shock for all the times we lean

our ears upon his mellow strength & thunder
. the lissom
jump from C-sharp-melody Missouri stomp

into up
-tempo country blues. the brown
preaching careless grace of the approaching Hawk

who now stands slow. ly in this London spotlight gaunt
& frail . whispy the lion hair & grey
the music he begins to pendulum so im

-perceptible it barely dream im
lips . the first notes whisp
-ering of something like the death

of all the certainties we'd known
. our use . our strength
. the wreckless way we race to wheel the tumbrils

of our future
now tumble down and sudden in this intimate inaugural
it seem he cdn't play at all god's creatures great & small

might not possess the strength to make his breath
swing into this curved placid plastic embouchure
and make it breathe

and sure. and make it shiver vivid like the towers
of his metropole now opening our ears to close our eyes to smiles
and bring us close together in a magic

only he cd cure
w/myrrh & anegeda salt & cinnamon upon our
flesh

And then the breath come back . slow . fall
-tering at first
and then it seem to calabash an unknown dangerous

light
far out on the horizon . fresh
wink/ing flights. a great fleet passing thru the fluent

night & upper air
a great tide rising rising rising ostinado up towards him on the band
-stand . tall

-er now. the saxophone xtending silver till it rounds
the golden horn . and its the Hawk again
and new . the soft cry rising feathers of all sound

around him . fold
-ing & unfolding as the chorus almost cock
-crow reaches us in this low distant New

York air beyond what we call age . infirmity . the loss
of el dorado . the para. box of para. dice . life
in this little rolling game of luck & toss-
ing chance canoe

For this is something other . some some-
thing else. far far beyond what we cd ever cd have known
about . x-

pected when we first hear the muse-
ic. think
that we know the muse

(s)' softly rage. ing snare & image & collage. think
that we share the man who make this muse. ic music
and that w/ the man-make madness in this swain

and autumn season. there wd be no decline from powvrs. our hex-
pectations now on full alert & almost all full-
fill(ed). not yet the un. xpecting hesitation. gilt. guilt

the liquid eyes seduce by lull & glitter
the pause before the keys begin to turn
the corner of the globe . and so despite the fall-
ing leaves of prayer . no wilt . no wilt . no flear

But this is something something something
other.   some some. thing else beyond the paradigm
far far beyond the limn

of para
-dice. that what we make. make well. may well
last long last long beyond the first breath fall

-tering. beyond the last leaves' last seeds' fall
-ing thru this london air. the thin
and hollow image of the Hawk

alone inside the spot
-light slowly filling out his shadow at the micro
-pole. the first limp

step. first first-step. first
-set legba notes of confidence. push
-ing aside the silence for the man to walk again on cool

laconic water. flex
-ing his knees to greet the feel
of his returning power

the petals. choradings. the dark magnolian roses
the changes. flare
-ing riffs

so that the bassist cd now settle into his familiar crouch & smile
-ing . the cymbal's *betcha* brass & chuckle radar
catching sight of where we are as we move on together to the fertile Nile

remembering becoming whole & powerful again
the bolgatanga baskets bountiful & fruit
-full oranges & rafts of sugarcane. fresh

juices tamarinda syrup half-way down the lane
the axe + àxé saxophone now simmering the room of smoky dark
-ness w/a glad

-ness we now know is stolen from our eyes by too
much inattention. drag & droop & dampness. blue
craft. less punishing despair

the broken quaver of the water leaking in our one canoe
perhaps our lass nice-time in london

•

but some day certain in the future of New
York. his magic enigmatic majesty now flower-
ing the room . his body glow-

ing *the only word we have* for what is now this glow-
ering around these future towers of his solo masterpiece
rising himself again in sound towards the silver cross

of an approaching jet. dissecting in the blue
the full white mosque and omen of the moon
just afternoons ago . high over Berkeley Square . over Washington Square

the body body body bodies pour-
ing from this dark Manhattan strom-
boli into dim catacoombs of dis-

appearing love & grace & pain & smouldering wound .
the crystal crash cenote. the crack-
(ed) styrated plates split spinning down from the dumb fumebellin volcano

their glass. their shattering in bleak & shackle runes
upon the masque & distant pelmet ground. the misty
singing from the ruin wells of wrackage. some somewhere some. weigh dun-

geon far off parfume failure of the ibis
this feed & promise
of a miracle . but not yet not

yet. altho we know it coming even while we count
the deed the dead the cruel lame the gnash the cost
the small the blind the debris falling from the air of shar

& lashes lashes lashes. such lash. erations of the hurt
& herd. the blunted flash & flint of oriole
& warp & timbrel flesh upon the manacle

flesh become salt. salt be-
come char & ruell achar ashes ashes ashes ashes
upn the lips upon my lids into this now curl-

ing cowl of howl & tears. the tears like bees upon my fingertips like bit-
umen. the sticky black the blurr the burn(ed) the bomb(ed) the scarr(ed)
the diamond. the people walk. in on their splashes hearts & living in the moon

and these here halt & scattered half-alive await it w/the risin g burkha dust
& monster all around us in this roar of wave and womb of rage now whispering
a coiled al'queeda & the long black stain of honey drowned before and under us

belovèds gone down in the daemon thunder-ridges
gone gone away down in the downward up. ward rush
of howling graveyard lava air . my little daring darlin daughters

o hero scream . Hiroshima . au quelle dommage
which Agent Ornage kora

blown w/their ribbons in. to the gutter's rush
their sweet red oils
staining the wide widening whitening side. walk(s)' slow
waken. ing nuclear midnight hush

knock. knock. in at the heaven(s) door

my Filenes Bargain Basement uncle
nvr going shopping there or anywhere so wonderful again. his cell-
ular titanium lip no more complain. ing from the 92nd Floor

we nvr find his body . we nvr find the phone
some somewhere in this wide gaping river of the city's
wound. he sits blind bound & bed. ouin in his seat of failure

we cannot even share the voice. less wire. less whisp-
er of his fate. not knowing if he jump. or burn
not knowing if he really still up there. or if he comin down

And so this foreday morning w/out light or choice
i cannot swim
the stone. i can't hold on to water. so i drown

i swallow left. i turn & fall-
ow into fear & blight. a night so deep it make you turn
& weep the line of spiders of yr future you see spinn-

ing here. their silver
voice of tears. their lid. less jewel eyes .
all thru this buffeting eternity i toss i burn

and when i rise leviathan from the deep . black shining from my skin
of seals. blask tooth. less pebbles mine the shore
haunted by dust & bromes . wrist. watches w/out tone or tides. communion

w/out broken
hands. x-
plosions of frustration. the trans-

substantiation of the sweat
of hate. the absent ruby lips
upon the wrinkle rim

of wine . i wake to tick
to tell you that in these loud waters of my land
there is no root no hope no cloud no dream no sail canoe or dang. le miracle .

good day cannot repay bad *night*. our teeth snarl snapp-
ing even at halp-
less angels' evenings' meetings' melting steel

in this new farmer garden of the earth's delights
this staggering stranger of injustices
come rumbelling down the wheel and grave-

yard of the wind. down the scythe narrow streets. clear
air for a moment . clear
innocence whe we are running. *so so so so so many*. the crowd flow-

ing over Brooklyn Bridge. *so so so many* . *i had not thought death
had undone so many* . melting away into what is now sighing . light
calp from the clear avenue forever

our souls sometimes far out ahead already of our surfaces
and our life looking back
salt. as in Bhuj. in Grenada. Guernica. Amritsar. Tajikistan

the sulphur-stricken cities of the plains of Aetna. Pelée. ab Napoli & Krakatoa
the young window-widow baby-mothers of the prostitutes .
looking back looking back as in Bosnia. the Sudan. Chernobyl

Oaxaca terremoto incomprehende. al'fata el Jenin. the Bhopal
babies sucking toxic milk. our growing heavy furry tongues
accustom to the *what-is-the-word-that-is-not-here-in-English* beyond *schadenfreude*
not at all like *fado* or *duende*

So what is the word
for this high rafter of suicide. the dove of the rope
choking the sweet cooing throat of the priests of success. the shock

of yr death in the fission of indebtedness
quagmire . darfour. waste. quick-silver into quick-
sand & chute. **My Brother**'s soft bowels of aids. the youth of the full taste of death

in the uncouth cooper of water .
what prophet my tongue
w/the tsunami loss of my Mother the Noun. the fail-

ure of falling angelicas' hope. alphabets stuff upside-down
in my mouth. bandaloo
babel. and the down-

fall of plaster upon all these voices & scores
dub rap hip-hop scouse. the lock-
chain(ed) markets of marrakesh

seething old sores
of no longer verbs
that can heal. of no longer baptisms

that will bawl out yr name from the top of disaster
adjectives already gone a-
way clattering. lounging in shame. the silence of rot

of the hot of unheavens. the dread kapot
ovens of the beast upon the thrashing floor of syphillis. flat
foot of fear . the unknown animal that is now yr sibyl sister at the door

the four
little bombard girls of Birmingham that ku
klux christian tabernacle night in Sodom & Herero

the corn
husk terror of Rwanda. the poor who live bom-
fim the stony guts & gashes of our or-

nate palaces. the roses widow now for. ever reach-
ing in frus. tration in her open-limmo fire-
crack. ing back. seat for her hero hero presidential husband's blown-

out confetti brains in Dallas
the curling Black Death mushroom gloam
of God in Nagasaki . what Pol Pot did

King Leopold's Great Pyramid. of Skulls inside the Belgian Congo
like judas come to chrissmas. like leopard come to lamb
even upon this dark un. even catastrophic ground where soon

the devastation saurus faces of the dead will dyaam us fron-
tom from their rat. tle sockets. the gentle liquid iris language of their prayers .
soft blades of cyandle eyes in psalms of pain & irie innocence .

of ruin photographs & childhood teddy bears' young lighted flickering hearts
against the black & shining iron railings' incense of the parks
all their birds

gone
leaves' spirits of green vegetation's ceremonies
gone

Rita Lasar Joseph O'Reilly Masuda wa Sultan. her 19 children
gone
the Ladder 16 Crew. *so many thousands*

gone
it look like nearly evva. one who went to work up they that way
is gone

like the day you make me swallow the tail of my tongue in the villages
following the foot-
steps of my own self my own self. the distress

of my own rivers of this flesh
mek dem kno wi feel
my own ash my own alph mi own outcry

how yu mek me sing these strange mesongs
in mi own *manteca* poem so far from music sex and saxophone
& nothing nothing nothing new

all wreck(ed) . all wrack(ed) . and
falling from the blue
Iran Iraq Columbus Ayiti & Colombo . Beirut Manhattan & Afghanistan

<

I was standin on the steps of City Hall . . .in all that dust

. . .

and I knew that Jerry [her husband the Captain of Rescue 11] wd have been

. . .

on one of the highest floor(s) that he cd get to. . .in that building

. . .

for that's what his Company does. . . and when I saw the building come down
I knew that he had no chance

. . .

Sometimes I start to worry that he was afraid. . .but. . . knowing him
I think he was completely focussed on the job at hand. . .sometimes it makes me angry

[she gives here a little laugh of pain]

but I don't think that he

. . .

I think in the back of his mind. . . he was more concerned about where
I was? and the fact that I was far-enough-away. . .from the trouble?
But I don't think that he considered. . . his not-coming-home

. . .

and sometimes that makes me angry. . .S'almost as if he didn't choose me. . .?
But I can't fault him for that he was doin his job. . .That's who he was
and why I lloved him so much

So I can't blame him for that

. . .

His friend Jim told me that he saw Jerry going in and Jerry said to him
we may not be seeing each other again
and kissed him on the cheek. . .and ran. . .upstairs [into the North Tower]

When the building came down

. . .

I just felt a complete disconnection in my heart

. . .

It was just like everything was just ripped-out-of-my-chest

. . .

I thought that Terry just

. . .

incinerated

. . .

I was grabbing the dust. . .from the ground. . . thinking that he was in the dust

Beth Petrone speaking in the HBO/TU Memorial Tribute to the Heroes of 9/11
(26 May 2002)
. . .for her own beautiful self . and for all the women of this poem's world in New York Rwanda Kingston Iraq Afghanistan. . .

I lost my husband . . .but I think that he did. . .the best that he cd

. . .

because I truly believe that when Jerry got to Heaven. . . he had so many chips in his favor that he bargained for this child because he knew that that wd be the one thing that wd save me

. . .

And. . . so I think in that respect(s)

. . .

I got. . .I. . .I . . .I'm go(ing) to live. . . I still have a part of Jerry

. . .

that I'm going to see in May. And a lot of apple people didn't get that

. . .

So I think that in certain ways. . .I was lucky . But in other ways

[and here she tries to smile]

. . . obviously. . .I was not. . .

[and makes a wordless Sorry]

>

so let us even at this time

remember the poor & the helpless the cold the hungry
les damnés de la terre

the sick in mind & body . them that will bear
the broken fence of mourning on their faces
the lame the lonely the unnamed unloving the unloved

the jaded agèd in the name of God . the little trace. less concertina children grain-
ering the wheatless streets of Rio Mysore Srebrenitza
none who will now nor know the living loving-kindness of the Lord
upon another shore

And the tune almost gone now from the solo
just its soft shimmering skein of archipelagoes
just walter johnson & the boys holding you up in this

pool & spot. light's shapely union
of yr pyramid . the fallow folded metal leaves un
-folding to the slow. down-spiralling bell & tenor

of yr song

& fallin here like sparrowes feathers sorrowes
o my love
but tall still tall from where you have been cast. cast

down the walls of pomp & pride & vivid firnament
the wealthy many-eyed & pixie prison-homes
come rolling down the rumble

of the tide of thorn & rock. et refuse. thrones
thrones thrown down a Babylon where you a-
bide. defile. so many lynching afternoons ago

strange etching fruit of lonely crucifixions' systemat-
ically broken hands & broken catatonic bones. so
many broken guitar strings. such kernel damage

in the white-tile bathroom precincts. the mush
gomorrah broom-
stick up. o curling Hawk. yr spoken haitian anguish

•

w/yr frail fierce solo
burning in the changeling light w/in this room so blue
so indigo

•

the feathers fall. ing fly. ing fall. ing fail. ing fall
ing in this new
new york monument of dying cold & aberfan

where so much glory has been pitch
& toss . green
sun so bright the shadows when you walk in them

are red & burn. ing thorn & muharram
. so many many children abikú & born
w/death. and their torn stories lost and nvr told

•

these chilldren mek
dis pack wit you
& yet they shoes lie
gape & laughin . emp-
ty blood-
(y) in the burn. in
grounn. . .

o come back Black Hawk
come back come back

turn
yr dark volume higher
up . let it plough
fields of patient terraces
again. long lonely roars
of corn for Ginsberg Whit-
man for Hart
Crane for Louis Ornette al-
ways for Rollins & for
Trane. for wind for
snares for turrets tunn-
els under-
wound & underground
& underriver. stair-
cases pour-
ing never-end-
ing down their space
w/no xit w/no amaz-
ing escape face no
save-
ing grace for all the
suns & mothers
of the murthered world
the headless heedless
streetless IIIWorld wo-
mans' infants aban-
don on hospital steps
in pothole sidewalks
full of spite. full law
on light-
less deconstruction sites
in gashes
at the sides of palaces
in signalling banana
leaves. the roll-
ingstock compartments
of our railway carr-
ages. in joy-
less bull-
rush rushes. in care-
full folded straw
the metal hearse
inside the mental horse
of Troy. three
hundred fifty firemen
them-
selves be-
coming fire. the glow-
ing shar-
coal engines of their
eyes still howl-
ing ishak me-
shak & abednegro

so now we live inside
this dusk
(y) afternoon . good

day i say again
cannot repay bad
night. our teeth snarl

snapp-
ing even at halp-
less angels in this

new dust
(y) garden of the
earth's delights

the sundered papers
from the world's
trades' tallest mon-

ument. these sun-
lit letters
of the spirit(s)

white litters
from the dead
of towers

bird stone flesh
pacsera. sera. pejarita.
and from the to be yet

un-
done un-
done

now sad
-ly flying some-
times soft-

ly some-
times some-
thing dizzy in the sudden knife

of sky
-light scalp-
less doves

like winkling stars'
disasters
in the life

of blue

.

even as you
comin . comin . warm konnu
like to the end of this long pull & palim

of yr song

shroud w/mirrors
haunted by showers
falling flowers

long before his time here flare-
ing future
where he arrives

this golden time
early like this
this early new york autumn season

.

ocol the cool the clear the towers falling
o let me
my belovèd

aXe

aXe

àXé

before these worlds falling clawes
i lose
u

these slacken broken doors of lawes
i lose
u

these words of love to sovereign wars of lust
to lose
u

even in the burn-
ing towers of this saxophone
o let me love you love you love you love you

vivid + green + golden

•

body

body & soul

in the performance or Audioglyph version of this poem. there shd be two murals corresponding in spirit
to the *marassa* (Twins) of the twin towers of the World Trade Centre . (1) of sound. grounded on Hawk's
Body & Soul' interacting w/among others. Duke Trane raga Adowa fado flamenço Billie & Nina ('Strange Fruit')
ghazal Tosh ('Fools Die') Thomas Tomkins qawwali Rachmanioff's *Concerto* w/postlude Marley's 'Ises' falling
shimmering & rising continuously behind the poem. And (2) the names of the belovèd dead so nommo in the poem
This double column of the ancestors will occur. their names spoken in all the various accents
tongues of speech of the bereave & falling falling on the audience like breath like leaves
like paper spirits of birds' feathers towards the very last & seaQuence of the moment/monument's beginning

Vii

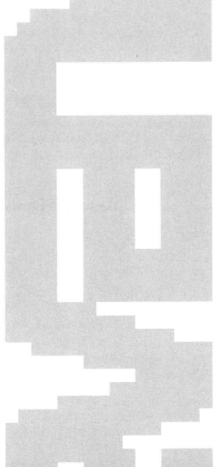

Namsetoura

From what far cost of Africa to this brown strip
of pasture on this coral limestone ridge
cast up some three miles from the burning sea.

the grave

hidden w/in the clump of prickly man
-peaba. red cordea trees
& countless clammacherry leaves

the spider warn me of her entry
trie to prevent my photograph
ruin three lenses brek down the hi-tec pentax

cameraderie

i click de pic
-ture w/ a simple borrow ko
-dax

it burrow thru the wave of dark & bring us this
past mid
-nights w/ yr silent humming

the musky smell of turning
in yr sweaty bed
the coir whispering of springs still centuries

away
no singing water in these wells
the cisterns dry

the empty moral memory for
-lone. its axe
head off. yr sweet mouth bash

& brutalize
my sister mother o my aunt my ancestor
the one eye sink away from her
-story

all down yr neck
along yr coral spine now welt
ing w/ the busha blows

yr back a modern mural
of dis
-tress. the whip of auctioneers

gold bangle blink
-in in yr ear. a takoradi nugget
in yr nostril

it is this other eye that blowes
my mind. wind
in a torch you blaze upon me from yr bale

-full stare. suns i have nvr known
worlds i can nvr nvr travel
in return

and yet yu tell me
this. yu tell
me. dis

no calabash or flower on my mound no nine night wake no forty days
of journey through the salt lagoon No
fruit to heal this lips No
okra at my hips. What happen hey to me

is like yu vomit-up a rodent in Kaneshie mar-
ket. Tree hundred years uh starin here under dis spider
web & bush.ananse at my door of herbs. an now yu come disturb
me wit yr camera destroy th ruin of my spiral

with yr flash. O watch me now. my chile my nephew
flesh great great grannbrudda from this other world.
Yu tink they dispossessin yu? Yu tink yu tall? you tink yu
mmassaccourraamann+rasta. boanurge? reckon yu rave?

Yu say yu writin poem about kimba slave Yu evva hear
wha GrandeeNanny tell de backraman a. bout she black back-
side? But looka yu doa nuh! Look wha he. come-a yu! mirasme buckra broni half-white back.
site bwoy. eatin de backra culcha. dah backra backsite culcha eatin yu

gyabiriw

Say wha?

De man yu say is man yu say doan unnerstann?
Too many christels in yr engine?
Yu brain like winnmill spinnin widout cane or agency?

De caatwhip cut yu tong?

Write dis in flash before de nex red season come
Doan write it down in coral
Dat is water Dat will spill
Write it inside my umfô body berry berry burnin coal

gyeNyamebiriw
gyeNyamebiriw gyeNyamebiriw

Gye only under God
the fire
but only from my bosomtwa

- yu tink i sick yu tink i slack - yo know whe bosomtwa? wha
call it so? - tell me why pig-snout long - why ratta live in hole -
- why nasty daag eat dutty puddin -
what is de cockroach fowlyaad sitiation?

gye only the redemption of my bosomtwa
mi tell yu

an de chilldren chilldren dis-yah wound
mi seh

//

ti

liberation

Ananse is the Akan Creator God. neglected/adapted/adire/re-adopted in the Caribbean/Américas. Namsetoura first appears @ CowPastor Barbados. th embattle home of Kamau Brathwaite, in September 2000. The *salt* of her nationlanguage is *barely* suggested here

The sacred lake of the Asante is Bosomtwi. Bosom means sacred & secret. **twi** is the name of the language. **twa** refers to the female sexual organ. In her 'presentation'. Namsetoura is very gesturally xpressive about this. She is able to combine all the meanings. in *vodoun. bosou twa/bosou twa kòn.* is a charm . fetish . talisman . mkissi

MOUNTAIN
for Philip Sherlock & those gathering for the K70 Golokwati at Mona Jan 2002

The great mass of the memory mountain
Long Mountain rise. ride up slowly out of the sea out of the time
before sun

-rise. even when it is dark. it is dark. it is home. it is here
the presences breaking thru light. which is still dark. which is still dark
which is still dark

-ness

.

i am not witness
-ing to anything like this. like this be
-fore. even tho i have seen islands breaking thru secrets

thru light . which is dark. which is dark. which is still dark
-ness. smudge. mark
clarion enough line on the horizon of what will soon be cliff

headland. ancient
distant dreaming volcanoes. mysteriously testament
drifting in cloud

.

but this *now* is *change*. is *now* is *change*
-ing. challenge
-ing home. approach

-ing unplangent & its perhaps potential & inevitable disaster
sweet
smell of soft star

-water under the cliffs. blue liquid runnings after the high
seas. not even a beach yet. no
canoes. no

sign of white or gold where we might
land. where we might walk far in
-land. or dip

& sun ourselves. figures in white walking slowly to baptism or balm

.

but still there is so much weight. so much grey awesomeness
ridges sharp like revenge . the silence
moving like comely cloud. like the great baobab

itself of the heavens. the land moving slowly like the great tree
like the leaves of heaven themselves in a great psalm. a steady serenity
. noise

-lessly certainty certainly. lights winkling above us. as if altho we still on
the ship. the same trip
on the water. we

-war Gap. breathing these frail moon duppe flowers
luminous cereus out of the mist. most delicate spiders
now orchid

-webs catching light in the trees. bird lizard
agate green diamond
memory of fire-

fly. of snapp
-ing periwinkle. sap
-ling. and pilgrim filigree of buzz of bees

how Newcastle sleep nvr slips down into Hermitage Valley. nvr reaches
Papine Mona Angola Tom Cringle Gate tho it is always there
looking down from its thunder. nvr reaches Wareika

too much dust these days there in that labouring bowl
too many gunshots & howl
-ing . the shriek. ing of bullets not green island shoots

how we have for too long now forgotten Count Ossie
his rasta drumbeats the waters of Kingston Harbour
his music the wide weeping wheel of the lap. the lap. of the harbour

& the landscape tuning to Kapo for houses. blue
& magenta boxes. black
borders. the quiet face of intuition painting in them

black doves w/fix wings plummeting towards groundation. shepherds
looking like Kapo himself
ancient egyptian natty bicycle riders even tho above them in babylon

already aground
in the house
of the ground. looking up at the sky but as yet w/out white faint

footsteps on the beach

that will reveal themselves as forest. as hope. as gong-gong yellow
blossoms of sound. green trees of the earth. out of reach
letting themselves cling to the mountain. lianas & climbing

.

already i can hear abeng & taitú. imagine the thin spine of the villages
smoke hawk dove Accompong
the now shallow of our ship like a whale in a shadow of water

even as we climb high
-er from its silence. sliding along the south
shore of the eye

-land. as the sun itself now breaks gentle
pink shell. blue fire. iris. eye rise of water. corona of blaze
ripping yr eyes across like the sea itself waking its white

rushing upwards its roar
tossed nodding indestructable parades thru the reef. its shackles
of violent sparks thru the dark cracks. pre

-histrionic granite & violet shade of the now rising John Crow Mountain
trails from its soft crest already Cinchona. spike
-nard of Hard

where there is already another terror of quarries
where the white footsteps have become cavernous gnashes
as if the whole mountain roaring w/shadows

as if the whole quandary roaring white tombs
as if the whole mountain roaring. leaving our chilldren alone in the hush
w/out incense

or license w/out innocence
w/out any pretences or prayer on the narrow rockstone path
-way of ambush

abena babena kukúma kush
yr narrow tunes & nuses
of dis. pair

But there are still rivers leaping into limestone
falls. Campbell's stone
-breakers (i telephone him this morning) how

Vic Reid write **New Day** . Philip Sherlock's Long
Mountain poem (so many dedications). Olive Lewin
leaning her tie-heading voices into Cane Garden flow

-ings. Bog Walk water gush. ings into cool Mahogany
Vales. soprano
birds. Landhovvery. old spanish walls. low alto

gleam of the cattle
pools. St Ann. the land of mahoe. of Paul Bogle's bugles
the rattle road

slippin down into showery
Bogue. in
-to Bull Bay where we pick plums. in

-to where in damp August Town
the Prophet Bedward will one day *dip dem dip dem dip dem*
closer to Redemption Ground

.

for we have love here beyond so much loss. beyond any previous
premonitions or promptings. along dry-river beds. among huge
white boulders long deserted by water. but still waiting still watchin

still holding on to the cool photograph of the mind
standing barefoot here on the land. sitting still in the wind. bend
-ing our soft ripple backs. washing. along fern gullies of water

little smooth-stone spirit footsteps across slippery rivers
bridges of spidery swinging suspending perilous crossings
MavisBank Rockfort Mocho RunawayBay walking the dust of the morning

Bryan Edwards' low lonely ranch they call castle. over
-looking so many miles of such tossing. sussurrus seas of green stalks
walking the wind. long branching silence plantations. path

-ways thru the grass. miasmri babies of rain in these poor huddle houses
slaves stamp from their past to this future forever horizon of pain
Edward Long. Rio Bueno

decapitations all thru the night at BlackRiver MileGully Morant
Bay. the hangings at Montego Bay. no
golokwati in sight till we reach Claude McKay's sad fiery apples of song

So let me sit. sit here still in this lonely but not alone
in the soft wind of prayer. in the first touch of the east
wind. mounting its trades of delight to the blue

all you
who have come smiling here to this place. greeting & welcome
placing yr gifts on the table

pause. sit. sip. take this small
bread of the moment. do
you remember?

bless this cool gourd of water
this likkle pinch of salamander salt
cowries are the tears of our lost love ones to keep faith with saith the Lord

yr warm & tallow cyandle
bodies touching each other in this gentle
grapefruit gift *mkissi* space out of harm's way. this simple grace

we seem so capable of when we ready leaning towards each other
& touch. ing even thru grilles
even tho we long-distance ourselves from the hills

creating these ghosts. these ghosts of beginning. first yellowy light
in the darkness. first light. light
-ly smoking out of the dews & the grasses. cool soft whistle

of first breath upon the dawn of yr first
film of skin. frost. silk. water. dew. the first opening whisper movement
of the world. making this difference that will now nvr end

because we here now. knowing each other at last & re
-membering. bring
-ing ourselves back from the dead

& the tumbril tumble down of what in another life seem like so
so much hesitation & failure. such a long waste of fallow
& flavour

but because we cd also do it this way
w/ such Eddie Baugh saying *it was the singing.* such body
-language & dreaming & nice-time

& saviour

that it makes this. this difference. something more tender than diffidence
tho there is that too. that here too
in the face of these spirits come down to the lyme of this room

of the moment among us & moving
among us. so far beyond the occasion. & lets us. allows us
into this silver mirror of journeys

so that we sometimes cast we sometimes cast
it over w/a soft blue cloth
of the spirits. hide our fears. tide of precarious tears

the little we have shored here brought to these least shores & cast
but not cast
down. not cast

away. cast
salt. cast
bread. this feast

-ing after these salt years of the fast
& in my palm a talisman. a tiny jewel fash
-ion to allow the dreaming on my shoulder

of so many other poets. such
little grace I carry I re
-ceive from you. from them. the way you write yr songs in

Cedar Valley brown. in
Miss Lou mallowing the anguish of the Inglish tongue. in
funde drum. in agave. in

joyful jump-up timbril castanet in
bood & dove guitar
in how the spirits speak in body-words & Kongo metaphors
the lilies lighted in the cotton-trees the seal the pencil ruler

scissors rising table shepherds. jeru & mu
sela selamawit adojinay
& Brother Single singkl-baibl dutty tuff in my jerusalem schoolroom

.

so as the almond tree proceeding thru its reasons
lights its translucent leaves. wet canvas green or slowly sailing blood
along the blue. the great white egret bird of morning riding air

& waning moon . from metal dawn to lateem sun
-sets flying thru their colours
cropover harmattan & hurricane & flood

from spider lilies' fading stars thru turquoise greens of days of sky & ocean
water blades' translucent grass the orange of the fruit & citrus sunset into
red & crimson indigo

So i turn back turn back to ship & journey here & water
flowing my beginning. quiet ending
the great mass of the memory mountain

rising up slowly out of the sea before sun
before sun
-rise

for even when it is dark. it is dark. it is home. it is here
the presences appearing thru the power thru the light. which is still dark.
which is still dark. the great fish underwater breathe. ing time

but w/the poem still largely unwritten really
the metaphors not properly in place
not properly the property of the poem

red riddims intervene/ing
w/too many other intertwining doubts too many clumping cloud
too too much lovevine still entangling the soar & soil

of my confession to the muse
too many fault-lines marking where I sorrow
craft & hurting heart & diligence of art

the poem 'finish' but not yet complete -
is yr compassion helping me to see
it. say it

so
whe all these unrhyme triplets nevva meet
tho some-a these-ya trophies & their lines read sweet

& now i know -
this has the poem & yr patience touch me teach me -
how god's things shift & change

thru high & low alone in crowds from continents to termites
of continuation but nvr lose their level vibes
their equal distribution in the universe

cane-cut or yam hill
fruit tree or bamboo juice. the sing it sing. it light
the steadily unfolding blessings of the land. how

we survive the midnight terrors when they knock or blow . fire
earthshake. know we the gunman of tornado when they blow. how
we survive the debt the acid

test. sun's dis-
affection. our daughters
on the street. all me can do is bann me belly when a feelin sick

& yet you bless. you bless me w/these hard. w/these hard-
working prayers of yr hands
yr maroon & Marcus Garvey rastafari fight for human rights & justice

in the world. that black & poor & dispossess are forces in the universse
like pride & passionate & knowin who yr folksongs are
o song so strong even in a strange land now yr own yr honeycomb yr hoom

▮

despite this ummark unattending in my verse
despite these mars that mark its making. even altho its wish
be pure. considering all the equal enigmatic aspects of the nation

.

& so altho i see the valleys. wild Wag Water prospects
& hear the water running in the rivers & along the shore
& even tho i reach the foothills. i do not know

that i will reach the mountains of tomorrow
tho i can see them. feel once more
the naked palm of feet upon my smaddy's sticky wooden kitchen floor

tho i give thanks & praises for what you have allowed me
helping me to find my space w/in yr welcome
& doing so i find myself inheriting this small important muddum
of yr grace

▮

for Zea Mexican

One late afternoon i drive AuntMay & DreamChad up to Hardwar Gap & the Park up there
Looking across from where we were there is a valley & beyond that on the same level w/us a <
wood in mist & you cd see a road & the light under the trees in the distance but it is like over <
there & you cdnt see the connexion how it get where it is how you cd get there & there was no
one over there there was no one over there Only peace As if ***there*** *is where she is walking away*
from us but perhaps waiting & each day gettin more & more involve w/what is happening over
there away from us & meetin the peopl out there & getting to know them & yr Mother event-
ually getting the Newes & setting out to find you in that landscape over there so near so far <<
far far away like the first hymn w/tears in it tears in its eyes so you cd hardly see the hill after
a time in the grey green going-down evening sun. light forever & for ever Heartease which is
where you are in this soft landscape distance shining and i am suddenly & at last happy & <<
very very sad & lonely bec ause you feel so lonely so lonely too & away but somehow at <
peace now forgetting/the-beginning-the-forgetting-and-the-always-always-remembering ***so <<***
you cd hardly see in the grey green going-down evening sun. light forever *you here we here <<*
you there we here and the sun almost gone now tho it shdnt and the peace however over it all <
all all it is gone & there is nothing i cd do any more nothing nothing nothing nothing i cd do <<
anymore nothing i cd ever do anymore but to lose you there & that way where i cd see & not
see you anymore beyond that valley high up here in the mountain shining shining shining in <
you thru all the peace & love & lovely seasons of the world

Robin

for Michael Kwesi & the blessing drummers of the lucumi

The mild blue
power-
line si-

ren song

•

catch
a robin w/a streak
of string

•

the white thread
catch
in the line

of song

•

curl
round the wire
and the rob-

in neck

•

and the bobb-
in bird on the drift-
in string

•

dang-
le all day
•

catch

in her flight's trans-
actions

power-
less breast
along the power-

lines' strength

•

The worry-
ing male bird
hear

the song
that the mild
blue power-

lines sing

•

an e come
to weep
where his catch

love life

•

hang

from the dang-
ling string

•

He flight
& flutter all the red
robin day

•

beatin his mourn-
in
feathers strength

on his blood-
red sun-
set wife

•

All thru the call-
ing home-
ward dusk

•

the mourn-
ing male bird circle
& sing

at the hope-
less
song-

less
tighten-
ing string

of his wife now
power-
less

love

•

But at dawn
next day a robin
cap boy

•

climb a ladder
& cut
the string

from the red-
head long-
dead bird

•

catch

the dark little mother that wing

•

and bury her love

KB/NYC Spring 02/Summer 04

NYC/August 04

KAMAU BRATHWAITE is born Barbados 1930 and educated there and at Cambridge [University] where he graduated in History 1953. He later returns to England (Sussex University & the British Museum Library) for his PhD (*The development of creole society in Jamaica 1770-1820* <1968; pub OUP 1971>. He received an Hon Doctorate of Letters from Sussex in 2002

Brathwaite worked (1955-1962) as an Education Officer in the Gold Coast/Ghana during its period of Independence, and while there developed (with his wife, Zea Mexican, at Saltpond) a Children's Theatre, that produced (1960-62), Pageant of Ghana, Edina, *Odale's Choice* (Evans 1968) and several *Anansesem* for Primary Schools (Longmans 1964)

He returns to work with the University of the West Indies 1962 (St Lucia) and Mona, Jamaica (1963-1991), with that break back to Sussex & London (1966-68) when, in addition to his PhD, he co-founds with John LaRose & Andrew Salkey, the Caribbean Artists Movement (CAM), and publishes the books of his first trilogy, *The Arrivants (1973): Rights of Passage* (1967), *Masks* (1968), *Islands* (1969). On return to Mona (1968/69), he continues the Caribbean Artist Movement as the journal & publishing entity, Savacou, which has now been extended (now Brathwaite is in N America <since 1990>) to SavacouNorth. It is during this time also that the books of his second trilogy *Ancestors* (*Mother Poem* <1977>, *Sun Poem* <1982>, *X/Self* <1997>) appear

What is so far less well known to readers outside the Caribbean, is Brathwaite's 'Time of Salt', as he calls it: the years 1986 -1900 which see in rapid catastrophic succession, the death of his wife Zea Mexican (1986), the destruction by hurricane of their home & archives at Irish Town in the high hills outside Kingston (1988) and his own death at the hands of brigand gunmen in his Kingston apartment in 1990, all chronicled in his largely new & strangely unknown groundbreaking << 'post-catastrophe' work - the third so far uncollected trilogy - *The Zea Mexican Diary* (1993), *Shar* (1990), *Trench Town Rock* (1999); a period which also witnesses, within these works and even more in *DreamStories* (1994), *DreamHaiti* (1995), *BarabajanPoems* (1994) and *ConVERSations w/Nathaniel << Mackey* (1999), the development of his 'Namsetoura/Sycorax Video/tidalectics Style', continuing in the 2-vol *MR* (Magical Realism <2002>), *Golokwati* (2002) and the New Directions edition of *Ancestors* (2001), which extend the boundaries of this writer's work far far beyond the 'definitions' of the first two trilogies thru which he is at present largely (un)known

His 'postSalt' poetry and 'dreamstories' may be found in *Words need love too* (House of Nehesi <2000>; new edition Salt 2004), in *Ark* (SavacouNorth 2004), and in the hopefully forthcoming *DS(2)* (New Directions) and *AmemPoems* (U California Press); and they should be read in the context of KB's post-Arrivants, postAncestors, postSalt work

Born to slow horses is the first major appearance in this country of this new (?4th phase) of Brathwait-(e)'s poetry; a work which in a sense, surveys or makes natural reference to the entire tidalectics, but at the same time marking, even with the most remarkable of his 'Caribbean' poems here, a significant transboundary development; continuing from *Words need love too,* perhaps another new tripartite exploration